How Can You Mend
A Broken Heart?

A memoir of finding hope and love in the midst of
abandonment, divorce, death, and fear

Kc Christman Hutter

innovo
PUBLISHING

Published by
Innovo Publishing, LLC
www.innovopublishing.com
1-888-546-2111

innovo
PUBLISHING

Providing Full-Service Publishing Services for
Christian Authors, Artists & Organizations: Hardbacks, Paperbacks,
eBooks, Audiobooks, Music & Film

A BROKEN HEART
Copyright © 2012 Kc Christman Hutter
All rights reserved.

Scripture quotations marked TLB are from the Holy Bible, *The Living Bible,* 1971, Tyndale House Publishers, Wheaton, Illinois 60187. All rights reserved.

Scripture quotations from *The Message.* Copyright © 1993, 1994, 1995, 1996, 2000, 2001, 2002. Used by permission of NavPress Publishing Group.

Scripture quotations marked NIV are from the Holy Bible, *New International Version,* copyright 1973, 1978 by International Bible Society. Used by permission of Zondervan. All rights reserved.

Scriptures quotations marked NKJV taken from *New King James Version Personal Study Bible,* copyright © 1990, 1995 by Thomas Nelson, Inc.

Library of Congress Control Number: 2012951484
ISBN 978-1-61314-068-0

Cover Design and Interior Layout: Innovo Publishing LLC
Photographs: Property of the author, Kc Christman Hutter

Printed in the United States of America
U.S. Printing History
First Edition: October 2012

~ Dedication ~

Remember, only one life and when it is past—only what is done for Christ will last! This book is offered up to the glory of God.

My dearest husband: Jerry loves me for me

My dearest son: Del loves me as Mom and friend

My dearest son: Cameron Gene loves me from heaven, and left me a blessed part of himself which lives on in his son, Cameron Cole

Don't fret or worry.

Instead of worrying, pray.

Let petitions and praises shape your

worries into prayers,

letting God know your concerns.

Before you know it, a sense of God's wholeness,

everything coming together for good,

will come and settle you down.

It's wonderful what happens when Christ

displaces worry at the center of your life.

Philippians 4:6–7 The Message

~ Contents ~

~ Contents ~

Section One

Twenty Miles from Home

~ 1 ~

I Know Who Is in the Box

Leafless trees look like frozen giants against the stormy North Dakota sky. Uncle Gerhard, Aunt Louise, and I drive into the churchyard. Windblown snow drifts over our feet. We walk the path and climb the stairs of the frosty white church. The inside, past the wooden doors, is as cold as the outside.

I shiver.

People are standing motionless in their black winter coats. The walls are pale grey. Christmas is next week—but there's no sparkle of tinsel anywhere, no smell of pine.

All of us Schmidt children walk to the front. Against the wall on the right side of the church, someone guides us to a long wooden plank. Five little kids sit close to each other for warmth. Our backs press tight against the wall. The church rumbles and groans in the blizzard.

I am eight-years-old and have lived with my aunt and uncle since my younger brother, Darrow, was born six years ago.

To my right sits my brother Russell. His birthmark is one white eyebrow—the other dark brown. Almost a teenager, Russ already resembles Dad.

I slide behind my older sister, LuJean, to keep warm and hide. She has blonde hair. Last fall, Aunt Louise and I drove to watch her tap dance at the Velva recital. Her legs kicked the highest.

People see me with Aunt Louise and say, "Oh, what a pretty girl—such big blue eyes."

I think of the big bad wolf in *Little Red Riding Hood*. The grandma said to the wolf, "Oh, what big eyes you have." The wolf replies, "All the better to see you, my dear."

My two younger brothers, Darrow and Gaylin, sit to my left. Darrow's chocolate brown eyes are set off by his skinny child's body. Little Gaylin's freckles are adorable.

I look around and see Aunt Louise, Aunt Esther, and Uncle Otto sitting in the pew. Tears run down the cheeks of my family.

Directly in front of the plank but more to the middle of the church sits a long wooden box.

My heart hurts and develops a small crack.

I know who is in the box.

Red Autograph Book

The church organ plays pretty music. We wait for the minister. I cover my face with an old scarf and try to remember.

A week earlier, Aunt Louise received a call from her brother, my Uncle Otto. "Louise, come to Minot. Albert and Dorothy have been in a car accident."

Aunt Louise and Uncle Gerhard loaded me into the car in the middle of the night. My brothers and sister were at home with a babysitter.

As we drove through the snow Aunt Louise told me, "Your mom and dad were passengers in their friend's car. When the car came down the Velva hill, a transport truck loaded with new cars crashed into it. The force of the truck hitting your dad's side of the car bent it into a V-shape. Your parents are in the hospital."

We arrived in Minot and my uncles and aunts took me to Dad's hospital room. Funny, noisy machines sat by his bed. Tubes came from his nose and mouth. A large tent hung over his chest.

One machine pumped, hissed, pumped, hissed. The dark hospital room reeked of alcohol, the stuff Aunt Louise pours on my cuts and scratches.

I cried and screamed, so the grownups did not take me to Mom's hospital room. Her body was also broken.

Everyone wanted to stay close to Dad and Mom, so we slept at Uncle Otto's house on the floor. He lives three blocks from the hospital.

During the night, the phone rang, the grownups cried.

I heard Uncle Otto say, "Albert is dead."

The conversation when Dad died: "He is in a better place— with his mother, Marie, in heaven. No more troubles."

Won't Dad miss us? Can Dad hunt and fish? When will he come and see us?

At the end of the funeral, someone opens the box. Dad is sleeping. He looks better than when I saw him in the hospital.

Cold ... c-c-cold me ... cold church. Should we find a blanket for Dad while he sleeps? I worry.

They'd postponed Dad's funeral twice because the doctors thought Mom might die. She is still in the hospital and can't attend the service.

The snowstorm still rages as relatives load the five Schmidt children into different cars.

No one is at home tonight at Albert Schmidt's house.

After the funeral I ride with Aunt Louise and Uncle Gerhard to their farm.

Is my room in their basement permanent? With my father in heaven, will I ever go back home and live with my mother, brothers, and sister?

Aunt Louise helps me move the table standing over the trap door in the kitchen floor. I pull the latch, the door opens, and I climb down the steep steps.

I shiver. No time to waste. In an old white dresser, I claw through clothes and look under my socks. At last—my red autograph book.

Eight months earlier, Dad had stopped at Uncle Gerhard's farm. We sat on the couch talking. I handed him a pen and asked, "Will you write in my autograph book?"

I can't remember his message. I flip the pages to find it.

April 8, 1950

Dear Karen,

Friendship is a gold chain of endless love and token, and Oh! my little girl, between you and me may not one link be broken.

Your Dad,

Albert Schmidt

* * *

One way of walking is head down and breathing through several layers of cotton scarves. I couldn't catch my breath, my lungs burned, and my eyeballs rolled around in sockets that felt like cold steel. I grew up on the flat plains of North Dakota.

We said, "Keep looking and you will see the back of your head."

North Dakota is a state of extremes. Watching a herd of Herefords grazing in green pastures, and their white-faced calves jumping in the spring flowers, was a peaceful sight.

Within twenty-four hours, that same herd could be ambushed by a sleet storm forcing them into a corner of the pasture. In the evening, they would stand with their butts to the wind. After a night-long storm, snow and ice would block their noses. They would be frozen, dead, standing with their eyes open. We were powerless against such extremes.

Little Green Tin Suitcase

People often asked, "Why do you live with your uncle and aunt? Your folks, brothers, and sister live close, why not live at home?"

"I don't know," I answered. Wondering, *am I a freak?*

I heard stories: Dad wanted his sister, Louise, to raise a child but she could not get pregnant. Mother already had four children and couldn't take care of the ones she had. Not enough food for the whole family.

Did my parents say, "We have four children, which one should we give away?" Or maybe they made their choice using the flower petal rhyme, "She loves us. She loves us not. We love her. We love her not." As I imagined the petals falling, I realized I'd always wonder.

I was driven away by my aunt and uncle. Sitting alone in the back seat, I looked out the window, tapped on the glass, and said goodbye. Tears dripped onto my little green, tin suitcase.

Don't Say a Word

One time Aunt Louise (Lou) and Uncle Gerhard (Gay) said, "Your daddy is going to pick you up today. Find your green suitcase, pack your pajamas. It's your sister's birthday."

LuJean's huge birthday cake was decorated with pink, yellow, and red flowers. Her friends, Diane and Kay, plus my brothers, Russell, Darrow, and Gaylin played "Pin the Tail on the Donkey." I laughed so much I almost wet myself.

When we went to bed, my sister and I crawled under a soft blanket. She reached under the bed and pulled out a small blue flashlight.

"Hold your hand in the light, make a dog head on the ceiling. Make him bark like this, open and close two fingers," LuJean said. We took turns.

I remembered to say my prayer, "Now I lay me down to sleep, I pray the Lord my soul to keep. If I should die before I wake, I pray the Lord my soul to take."

"LuJean, I don't want to die tonight." She didn't answer. I rolled on my side and hugged her.

The next day Lou and Gay picked me up from Mom's house. Lou looked back at me from the front seat. "Did you have a good time? Get a bath? Or did the witch spank you?"

"I had a good time. LuJean and I took a bubble bath in the big white tub with a yellow duck and toys." We didn't have a bathtub at Gay's farm.

I watched the countryside as I sat alone in the backseat. Stones kicked up underneath the car as it rolled down the gravel road, everything and everyone else was quiet.

Do not say a word. They might feel bad if I tell them I want to go back and spend another night. Maybe get jealous. Dad didn't invite them to LuJean's party.

* * *

The Sunday school teachers at St. Olaf Lutheran Church decorated a very large evergreen tree for Christmas.

In Sunday school we sang, "Jesus loves me this I know, for the Bible tells me so."

Someone loves me: Jesus. This thought gave me a good feeling. *I'm not alone and somebody loves me.*

All the children received a brown sack of goodies at the church's Christmas Eve service. The contents included a couple of unwrapped chocolates with sweet white centers, an apple, peanuts, and nuts. I carried the sack around until the last nut was cracked.

On Sundays, big families filled the pews in front of us. Brothers and sisters whispered and passed notes. I observed all this family activity.

"Lou, one Sunday can my sister come to church with us? LuJean and I will be good and not pass notes or talk."

* * *

It was sixty-seven years before I got any explanation as to why I did not live with my family.

My sister and I were visiting Aunt Jean, my mother's eighty-six-year-old sister, in Phoenix.

Aunt Jean sipped her tea. "Karen, your grandmother Marie Schmidt was a real witch. She, together with Albert and Louise, outranked your mother. Your mom and dad had two children. Then Dorothy became pregnant with you, her third baby. Since Louise didn't have any children, they schemed against Dorothy. When she went into labor with her fourth baby, you were to go and stay with Louise and her husband, Gerhard. They would keep you. You were less than two years old."

Pouring another cup of tea, Aunt Jean continued. "The old homestead at Strawberry Lake housed three families and they all shared one kitchen. Your mom, dad, and you kids all slept in one bedroom."

My older sister, LuJean, jumped into the conversation. "I remember chairs being raised by Dad and slammed onto the floor, shattering into many pieces. Mom and Dad fought about you not coming home. He won. You lost. You have to remember Dad was seventeen years older than Mom. Our brother Russell was born right after she turned seventeen."

* * *

When I was little I didn't know living with Aunt Louise and Uncle Gerhard was Dad's decision. It confused me: *Why didn't I go home to live?*

I remember wondering after Dad died: *When Mom recovers from the car accident will she bring me home? I'm tall, eight-years-old and have pretty blue eyes.*

Mom never drove her Chevy Impala the twenty miles to get me. Instead, she remarried and gave birth to three more children. *Who would love me now?*

Dad died; Mom remarried. Aunt Louise and Uncle Gerhard never said, "I love you."

I'd better be good. Lou and Gay might get tired of me and want to give me to someone else.

It gave me comfort to read in Sunday school about how much God loved me.

Hope for the Dark Days

For if my father and mother should abandon me,

you would welcome me and comfort me.

Psalm 27:10 TLB

Don't be afraid, for I have ransomed you;

I have called you by name;

you are mine.

Isaiah 43:1 TLB

Truck-Car Collision Kills Ruso Man Here Friday

The car accident in which my dad (Albert) was killed and my mom (Dorothy) was seriously injured. [photo December 14, 1950, courtesy of *Minot Daily News*.]

The only picture I have of my daddy holding me. My mom is holding Darrow. LuJean and Russell standing in front.

The Schmidt children: (*left*) Russell, LuJean, me (Kc), Darrow, Gaylin (1950).

~ 2 ~

Farm Girl

My friends were Brownie, Molly, Happy, Bimbo, Pal, Tiny, Darkie, and Freckles—my pets. Tiny was a short-legged, little, brown dog. For the Turtle Lake Parade, I led him through the streets as he pulled a small wagon. We looked so cute the judge gave us a red ribbon.

One day Tiny followed me to school—and then I never saw him again. A neighbor accidentally struck and killed my dog. The man picked Tiny up, loaded him into his car, and took him to Gay. They buried him.

When I came home from school Lou said, "Don't worry, Karen, your dog now lives with the Lord and Grandmother in heaven. They are better off."

* * *

My brown mare, Molly, had a fat back—straight as a board. I stood tall on her back while she galloped. We performed like a circus act.

One day I led Molly over to the wall in the barn where Gay kept her harness. At nine, I wasn't tall enough to reach over her back. I climbed the wall and hung off the wall hooks. Somehow, I wrestled the harness onto Molly.

I'd watched Uncle Gay build a stone bolt sled, a flat wooden platform nailed to runners. It was used for hauling stones out of the fields to improve the plowed land.

Grunting and groaning, I hooked the soft leather harness to the stone bolt sled.

"Karen, who helped you harness Molly?" Lou questioned. She couldn't believe I had accomplished a man's job.

"I did it all by myself," I said.

Then finding a white kitchen chair and placing it on the stone bolt sled, I jumped on the chair.

"Giddy up," I said, gently guiding Molly with the reins, as my chair became my make-believe throne and the stone bolt, my chariot. We stopped and loaded small rocks onto my one-horse open sleigh.

Freedom of Flight

One crisp fall day, I rode Molly to a neighbor's farm. There were many pets on our farm but I was still lonely.

"John, we drove by your farm on the way to Turtle Lake. A flock of pigeons was circling your barn. Gay told me I could raise pigeons. Could you spare a few?" I asked.

"You may have as many as you want. Come back in the evening, the birds will be roosting and you can help me catch them," John said.

I rode Molly back to the Walker farm in the evening, gunny sack thrown over my shoulder.

"Shhhh," John said, holding his finger over his lips.

We entered the barn. We spotted the white and black pigeons with a flashlight.

"John, up there, the dark brown one," I whispered.

Gently, we placed seven birds in my sack.

I rode Molly home very slowly. No bouncing the birds. The pigeons were secured in a vented box for the night.

The next morning I was so excited I could not eat breakfast. I needed to build them a nest out of apple crates.

"Karen, try nailing each box open-side up in the chicken coop," Gay said.

With hammer, nails, and wood stacked under my arm, I walked down the hill to hang the crates.

Within a few years, a beautiful flock of black, white, brown, and spotted pigeons circled our yard. Watching new babies test their wings, I dreamed about the freedom of flight. It is safest for birds to be in the air—too close to the ground they are exposed to predators.

They're just like me, so often I feel exposed—and alone. Lord, there has to be someone in this world made just for me. I know You love me. Please Lord, I need to hear "I love you" out loud. I need someone's arms to reach around and hold me.

One-Room Schoolhouse

On warm days, I walked the mile to school. If I crossed the pasture, took my shoes off, then waded thru the stream, it seemed shorter. I never got my shoes wet because wet shoes meant a spanking.

We had rules at Gay's house: In the winter, you never, ever, open windows. When you go in and out of the house, don't lollygag. Shutting the door fast keeps the house warmer.

One of the first days of school, I said to my uncle, "Do you want to bet a dime I am the smartest kid in my class?"

"Do you study hard?" Uncle Gay asked.

"No, it's because no one else is in my grade this year. Ha ha ... all alone." I told this joke many times.

Some years, my friend Elaine's school didn't have a teacher. When this happened her parents drove her to my school. Elaine's presence made class better because then the teacher had two kids to holler at, not just me. One year, the one-room Kalland School set a record high with fourteen children attending the multi-grade classroom.

Pump-Pump-Pull-Away

Everyone in school was looking at me. My body shook. This game was scary. I knew the kids would be running toward me and I felt wonderful and important.

"Pump-Pump-Pull-Away" made me so happy. The kids actually listened to what I said. Someone noticed me!

I screamed, "Pump-Pump-Pull-Away, run or I'll pull you away!" Ten, eleven, I don't know how many kids started running.

I was in fifth grade and two of the boys playing were big eighth graders. My legs were shorter but I still caught them. Everyone tried tagging the red barn. If I touched them before their hand hit the barn, they were on my team.

On my way home from school, I noticed holes in my pants. I should have been more careful.

"What on earth happened to your pants?" Aunt Lou asked.

Excitedly, I answered, "We played this game at noon hour. One kid stands in the middle of the yard and yells, everyone runs. Dennis, you know, Dennis, the eighth grader, I caught him. I want to play this game all my life."

Lou smiled at me which was good. She was not mad at me anymore and would fix my school pants and not scold me.

* * *

On cold winter days, I wrapped my head in layers of scarves to ride my horse to school. Lou laughed at my eyes peeking out.

When I was on Molly's colt, Darkie, it was dangerous to ride alongside the Keel boy and his horse. One morning, they took off galloping. Darkie followed chase and soon bucked me off.

I screamed, as my body flew through the air, "Help!" I landed headfirst in a snow bank, unable to breathe.

The Keel boy turned his horse around immediately. "Where are you?" he called out. He spotted my boots sticking out of the snow and pulled me out. We were late for school.

"My neck and tummy hurt," I said to my teacher.

"You may lie down on your coat in the corner if you need to," Mr. Edwards said.

I complained as soon as I arrived home after school. "Darkie bucked me off on my way to school. My neck and tummy are hurting."

Lou rubbed alcohol on my neck. My injuries from the fall amounted to a painful lump on the back of my neck and a protruding rib bone which was never wrapped.

* * *

In the winter we'd eat our school lunch quickly, and then head for Lake Nettie. We took turns on the toboggan or sled. Our throats hurt from all the screaming. We climbed up the hill, over and over, faster and faster. On some runs, the sled was going so fast we'd end up way out on the lake. Why couldn't noon hour have lasted three hours?

The school bell rang. We had ten minutes to run to school, take off our wet, top layers of clothes, and sit down at our desks. All of our mittens, coats, scarves, and sweaters were hung around the old stove. The icky, burning wool smell stunk up the schoolroom.

Reading the Sky

Winter temperatures could fall from forty-above to forty-below within a few hours. An absolute temperature range record for the Western Hemisphere was set during 1936 in North Dakota. The temperature went from minus 60°F to 121°F above in the same year. On white-out days, we couldn't even see our hand when our arm was outstretched.

"Follow me, hang onto the rope behind me," Gay said, tying one end of rope to the house. At the barn, he tied the other end. On our way back, we followed the rope to the house. Strong icy winds stung our cheeks and forced our eyes closed.

Gay told me more than once when I complained about the cold, "This is God's country—our climate keeps the riff-raff out."

Who is the riff-raff? I knew they must be bad, maybe even Republicans.

Uncle Gerhard, a die-hard Democrat said, "The Democrats vote for farm programs, they're for us poor folks."

* * *

On Friday nights, we'd travel to the neighbor's house and play cards. About midnight, after coffee and snacks, we'd start putting on our coats. For some unknown reason, this always triggered a several-hour political debate.

Our Republican neighbor, John, and Uncle Gerhard stomped their feet, raised their voices, and argued until their faces turned bright red. Fully dressed in my warm winter coat, scarf, and boots, I'd fall asleep on the floor by the door. The next Friday night, it would be a repeat performance.

Gay and Lou played cards with really old people whose children were grown up. When they were short a person, I filled in. My eyes watered because of the cigarette smoke. Every corner of the table held over-flowing ashtrays.

One winter night, the grownups didn't need me to play whist. There were three tables of card players. One table was in the bedroom. Bored, I crawled under the big coats piled on the bed. No one saw me, nor heard me.

John said to those playing at the bedroom table, "I don't think they arrested the right man for the Wolf family murders. People think maybe it was the two drifters from Canada. One man couldn't have killed the Mrs. and Mr., plus their five daughters, and the hired man. Their baby girl was the only one found alive. She had been crying for three days in her crib. A neighbor stopped and found the terrible mess."

"Things like this never happen around Turtle Lake," added another person.

Coats over my head, I stuck my fingers in my ears. I didn't want to hear the gruesome story. They were all shot. The police found one of the girls, who was my age, in the pig pen half-eaten.

If I die, I hope it is not because someone shoots me. It must hurt.

Lou and Gay didn't want me to know about the murdered family. I wasn't trying to eavesdrop, just trying to sleep. I never wanted to be left alone again. When Lou and Gay went to Turtle Lake without me, I'd hide in the house.

*If the man comes into our house with his gun, he won't find me.
I will be hiding under the bed in the basement with my flashlight.*

* * *

One night, while Gay was playing cards, I noticed the coloring of his fingers. The next day I asked, "Why are the tips of those two fingers brown?"

"Oh," he said, rolling a thin cigarette from the tobacco in a Red Velvet tin, "these two fingers are used for holding my ciggee butt."

In the evenings, he rolled cigarettes. He lined up the little tobacco soldiers in rows on a TV tray. In the morning, he hacked, coughed, and spit. Grabbing his cup of strong black coffee, he would light his first "ciggee" of the day. A grey cloud with a distinctive odor followed him around the house. Stinky smoke signals were left behind in the ash tray.

* * *

When the landscape was brown and bare, it took only one cloud of rain to bring the land back to life and put leaves on the branches. We retrieved our laundry from the clothesline when clouds banked up on the horizon. I learned to read the sky.

Now, when buying a house, I always choose one on a hill. "Don't hem me in and don't block the view" are my theme song. And I still think: Rain! Quick! Get the clothes in.

Hope for the Dark Days

What a beautiful home, GOD of the Angel Armies!

I've always longed to live in a place like this,

Always dreamed of a room in your house,

where I could sing for joy to God-alive!

Birds find nooks and crannies in your house,

sparrows and swallows make nests there.

They lay their eggs and raise their young,

singing their songs in the place where we worship.

Psalm 84:1-3 The Message

Strength! Courage! Don't be timid;

don't get discouraged.

God, your God, is with you every step you take.

Joshua 1:9 The Message

Kalland School, one-room schoolhouse (grades 1-8), near Turtle Lake, North Dakota

Me and Darkie. I raised and trained him as a colt and he still bucked me off.

~ 3 ~

Childhood Life on the Farm

The sun scorched the sod as I sat on the tractor in a cloud of dust. *Where is Lou? Sure could use water and lunch.* Finally, I could get out of the hot sun and into the shade of the tractor tire for food and a much needed rest. Lou left me the Ball glass jar full of ice water.

Uncle Gerhard needed a farm worker. I had three brothers living at my mom's home—maybe he should have picked one of them. Since I lived with him, I qualified for the job at the age of ten.

Plowing up the stubble fields of black moist dirt, a pungent earthy odor filled the spring air. Sea gulls followed the plow diving for mice, gophers, and bugs. I called them "Country Gulls."

Gay bragged about me, "Karen's the best tractor driver. She does everything except drive the big combine. Cultivating corn, her corners are perfect. She never cuts down any standing corn stalks."

Watching the swatter cut grain in the fall, I'd dream that the long-stemmed wheat fields waving in the wind were ocean waves. I'd never seen the ocean but I had a rich imagination. *Someday, I will be living and walking by the ocean!*

Cutting and then stacking the alfalfa in the fall were my favorite jobs. The cool air, smelling like honeysuckle and wild flowers, lingered in the freshly cut meadow. The blue sky turned bright gold, red, and orange, ushering in the evening glow of fireflies.

"Gay, I'm cutting a bouquet to take to Lou," I said, rolling up my pants and wading out into the water. The alfalfa field weaved in and out around a small pond full of pussy willow and cattail.

Arriving back at the farm, dusty and tired, I handed Lou the old silver pail.

"Beautiful," she said, "thank you." And she placed the gift on an old varnished table in the middle of the living room.

* * *

Aunt Louise had a butcher's knack for cutting the heads off fowl. Duck, goose, grouse, pheasant, turkey, Rhode Island Red chickens, or heaven forbid, even my pigeons appeared on our dinner plates.

"Can I pick out the dessert?" I would holler as I climbed down the steps to the fruit cellar. Lovely jars of home-canned fruit were displayed on rows of shelves: crab apples, Bing cherries, pears, and peaches all waiting to be devoured. My choice: Bing cherries.

My aunt was a cook, baker, butcher, seamstress, nurse, Sunday school teacher, and wife. She also whipped up interesting concoctions in the kitchen.

I screamed, "Ouch, it burns!"

Louise came running. "What's wrong?"

I pointed to the cake pan filled with white square bars. The piece lying on the table was missing one bite. "My mouth, my mouth," I said, choking.

"Not fudge! Lye soap," Louise said as she grabbed me and poured a glass of milk. "Here, drink, gargle, spit." My mouth was red and full of blisters for many days.

* * *

"Karen would you like to learn how to sew?" Aunt Lou asked. She wanted to keep me busy during long winter nights.

"Sure, I'll try."

For Christmas, Lou gave me seven washed, flour sacks. These were mine to embroider for my hope chest. The corner of each towel named one day of the week with a picture of a woman doing some type of household chore. The Monday towel was a woman washing clothes; Tuesday, ironing clothes; and so on for each day of the week. On Monday we didn't always wash clothes. We worked around the rain and snowstorms. Wind dried the clothes. When it was below zero, the clothes froze and hung stiff like boards on the outdoor line. The thought of crawling into bed with sheets smelling of fresh air and sunshine made it worthwhile.

Lou and Gay had hope—more rain, fewer severe rainstorms. "Please, God, no hail." A ten-minute hailstorm could wipe out our income for the whole year.

Money or no money, our old Chevrolet sat in the parking lot at St. Olaf every Sunday—the three of us in the pew.

Every fall Lou said, "Maybe next year we can build an entry room for the winter coats and muddy shoes. Building the steps to the basement outside and sealing up the trap door in the floor would give us more floor space in the kitchen."

In the spring, the only money left needed to be used for buying baby chicks, seed for the crops, and gas for working in the field.

School Bus Girl

The faded yellow school bus stopped at our mailbox. My plaid skirt bounced up and down as I ran down the driveway and boarded the bus. The driving time to Turtle Lake from the farm was twenty minutes. The first day of high school, with all the bus stops, the ride took over an hour.

My clothes were second-hand or homemade by Aunt Louise. The dress style during my high school years was a short-sleeved dress, belted around the waist, and either a full or straight skirt.

Uncle Gerhard exploded the day I took the belt off my dress. "It looks like you're trying to hide something. Go back and put on your belt. People might think you're wearing maternity clothes," he said.

It was normal for girls ages one through ten to swim in our underwear. If boys were around, we would leave on our shirts. My freshman high school year, Lou ordered a one-piece black swimsuit with red and blue horizontal stripes from the Sears, Roebuck, and Co. catalog. A cord around the neck held the suit up. My first new swimsuit—sweet.

On the last day of school of my freshmen year, we had a picnic at Crooked Lake. My classmates and I tossed a ball back and forth in the lake. I reached up to catch the ball and down came the top of my swimsuit. I never realized the cord around my neck would stretch when it got wet. My chest was exposed!

Some senior girls noticed the accidental display and splashed over. "Karen, jump up, we want to see your cute swimsuit," one of the girls said.

Embarrassed, I quickly left the picnic.

* * *

Watching cheerleaders at basketball games, I wanted so much to be one of them. During my freshmen and sophomore years, Lou didn't want me to show off my legs at the games, so I didn't try out.

My junior year, I begged Lou, "Please let me try out. It would be exciting to be on a squad."

"OK, you can be a cheerleader if the skirts are not short," Aunt Louise said.

"The skirts are long, to the knee."

I made B-squad and was thrilled to be part of the action. The girls cheering with me were freshmen and sophomores. I was proud to be part of the group, it didn't matter that I was the oldest. Life seemed perfect.

The summer before my senior year, all I thought about was cheering on the A-squad. On the farm, I practiced cheers by myself, jumped, ran, and stretched. The other girls were from town or lived close enough to each other to practice together.

Finally, the big day arrived. Students were in the gym. My heart almost jumped out of my chest. My turn. Smiling, running to the middle of the gym floor—a perfect cheer: "Turtle Lake Trojans, Rah, Rah, Rah" ending with an extra high jump. Not good enough, I made B-squad.

Oh, the tears! Ashamed! There's no way I would enter the girl's dressing room now. I was too disappointed and embarrassed. I found Mrs. Jacobsen, our advisor, and told her, "I can't be on the B-squad with the freshmen girls. I'm a senior."

She withdrew my name. This definitely qualified as my saddest day of high school.

Faye, my best friend, told me the girls sitting around her voted for me. I found out later that I'd lost the A-squad position by one vote.

After the cheerleading tryouts, the yellow bus ride seemed one hundred miles long instead of twenty. I sat alone in the back with my hood up.

My freshmen year, I met a boy from Butte, a town twenty-five miles northeast of Turtle Lake.

Delmer was good-looking with dark brown hair. His pleasant easy-going manner intrigued me.

Wearing his ring around my neck on an old black metal chain indicated we were going steady. I didn't go to Turtle Lake school dances or parties, never kissed another boy. I missed out on a lot of fun at school functions. But spending my nights alone, when I couldn't be with Delmer, was my choice.

Lou and Gay approved of Delmer because he attended the Lutheran Church, and didn't smoke or drink. They would not let me date a Republican or a Catholic.

The only advice Louise gave me about men, "Karen, don't ever say you are hot. Men will get the wrong idea. Just say, you're rather warm."

I must have been well-trained, I'm still just: rather warm.

* * *

In the winter, the roads were blocked by snow, so the country students stayed in town during the week.

Finally, during LuJean's last year in high school, we lived together for a few months. Our fantastic little two room basement apartment seemed like a castle. We laughed and talked into the night. She read *True Romance* which contained hugging, kissing, and heavy necking.

I didn't dare take the romance books to the farm on

weekends, Lou might find one. On Friday nights, LuJean went home and I went to Gay's farm.

I admired her—my very own sister. During those months, LuJean taught me things I should have learned from Lou.

* * *

Graduation, the big day, was six months away. I started leaving clues, "Most of the girls in high school have watches with wide bands."

The evening before graduation, Aunt Lou and Uncle Gay handed me a gift box. I shook it.

Better be careful and not break the watch before it's worn. Please Lord, just one dream fulfilled.

The wrapping from the box lay on the floor. Inside the box, a sparkling necklace from the local drug store.

Money or no money, I don't care! My heart yearned for a watch.

I pulled the latch of the cellar door and retreated.

Good Girl

Uncle Gerhard and Aunt Louise demanded perfection. I tried to be perfect—a good girl. I attended Sunday school,

Luther League, was baptized and confirmed, and played piano or organ for church and Sunday school events.

I never swore, talked-back, drank, or screwed around with boys. Everything I learned in Sunday school, I took to heart. I do not remember a time I did not believe in God. His commandments were written on my heart.

Bad Girl

During my senior year, one night my boyfriend and I pulled into our driveway at 1:00 a.m. We were not worried about the time. Garrison was an hour's drive from the farm, plus the roads were icy. I don't remember the movie. What happened when we arrived at my house, I would never forget.

A North Dakota blizzard raged. Delmer never walked me to the door. He drove his Chevy into the circle driveway, let me out, and continued around the house. Then quickly, he headed back for his home in Butte. I pulled my long scarf around my neck and ran to the front door.

Before I turned the knob, the door flew open. Shocked, I looked down the barrel of a rifle.

Uncle Gerhard roared, "Get in this house! Anything that happens after midnight is bad—no good, no good at all. Where in the world have you been?"

"To the movie in Garrison." I spit out the words.

Uncle Gay wasn't pointing the gun at me anymore. Lou, coming into the kitchen, said, "Albert should never have married your mother just because she was pregnant."

Words were fired at me fast. With the rifle still in Gay's hand, I couldn't think. I wanted to tell them I wasn't doing the F—word. I considered the word very bad and didn't have the guts to say it out loud.

"Your mother never loved you. I spent time at the lake home when you were a baby. She never changed your wet diapers. Instead, Dorothy stood over you, rubbing her two fingers together, saying, 'shame, shame on you, you bad little girl. Hush, you hush.' Your mother never picked you up. You cried and were wet all day," Lou said.

"Next time you go to a movie, come right home. Mr. Beggs told us he saw the two of you in Delmer's car parked on an approach," Lou continued.

Many times I had heard Lou talk badly about my mother. She hated her. I don't ever remember Gay being so worked up.

I don't know who left the kitchen first that horrible night. *How could they feel this way about me?*

My eyes hadn't yet closed in sleep when I heard the alarm clock ringing upstairs. Quickly dressing for church, I picked up my small black zippered Bible, and went upstairs, ready to go. As we drove to church, I tapped my fingers on the window watching the farms streak by. I felt totally alone and afraid. No one ever brought up the conversation of the night before—or the gun.

Thank you for defusing the situation last night, Jesus. I'm doing my best to be loved here on earth. I treasure Your words to me.

After high school graduation, I wanted to become a stewardess. Traveling to see the world and getting paid to do it, seemed so glamorous. The only trips I'd taken so far were by car, truck, or train—to South Dakota when I was four; Montana to a Luther League camp; and one fishing trip to Canada. Gay, Lou, and I had several conversations about this and about attending Teacher's College.

Money seemed impossible to accumulate. I worked as Gay's hired-hand in the summer, twelve hours a day, for my room and board. I had no money of my own.

"I don't want to worry about you up in the air. Planes crash!" Lou said. She nixed the stewardess career choice.

Even if I could have found a way of working in Minneapolis and paying my way for stewardess training, it was more important that Lou and Gay didn't hate me.

My sister attended Minot State Teacher's College. LuJean told me she worked for a doctor and made enough money for college. I would have liked to live in Minot near my sister.

Aunt Louise read to me out of the *Minot Daily*, "College students get drunk and streak nude at the football game." She added, "You can see Minot is a loose, party city. You better not go there."

I respected their decision. I knew they had both been pulled out of school before the sixth grade to work on their parents' farms. They worked really hard to keep food on the table. I didn't want to add pressure to their lives. They were proud I graduated from high school.

For six months, I attended Capitol Commercial Business College in Bismarck. Again, I found myself under someone else's control. No money for an apartment, I lived with a rich couple and worked for my room and board. Their English Tudor home looked like one right out of a magazine: six bathrooms, carpet, and a dirty clothes chute from the top floor to the laundry room on the bottom floor. To get to my room in the basement, I had a door in the wall, not in the floor.

The first week at my new home I prepared dinner and called, "Kids, come and eat."

Four-year-old Gretchen answered, "We are not kids, we are children. Kids are goats!"

Never had this been explained to me before. And at my age, I was thankful Capitol Commercial offered a Nancy Taylor Finishing Course. I found out that some tables are set with more than one spoon. *Big world out there and I want to be part of it!*

Hope for the Dark Days

Trembling and horror overwhelm me. Oh,
for the wings like a dove, to fly away and rest!
I would fly to the far off deserts and stay there. I would flee to
some refuge from all this storm.

Psalm 55:5-8 TLB

The character of even a child can be known
by the way he [she] acts—whether
what he [she] does is pure and right.

Proverbs 20:11 TLB

Fear not, for I am with you.
Do not be dismayed. I am your God.
I will strengthen you;
I will help you; I will uphold you
with my victorious right hand.

Isaiah 41:10 TLB

Section Two

To Be Loved Here on Earth

~ 4 ~

Set Apart for This

I graduated from high school in May 1960 and married Delmer in April 1961. A beautiful boy, Delbert, was born on July 8, 1962. I'd dated Delmer for five years and was a virgin when we married.

Why the rush?

"You better get married or try getting a job. No money for college," Aunt Lou told me.

You just don't know any better when you are from the plains of North Dakota. I guessed if I didn't get married now, I would be an old maid.

A second baby boy, Cameron Gene, was born in 1965.

I prayed many times as a young girl, "Lord, if you grace me with children, my love for them will be unconditional. I promise to take them to Sunday school, church, and make sure they are baptized and confirmed. I will also make sure they know how much You love them. I will tell them every day how much I love them, and give them lots of hugs and kisses."

Born on the Corner

After Delmer and I were married, we wanted to go to Mexico but I needed my birth certificate to travel out of the country.

Mom told me, "When it was time for you to be born, Albert drove me to Turtle Lake. On the corner by the Farmer's Union Station stood a small house. The mid-wife, who owned the house on the corner, was Mrs. Corner. You were born at the Corner's house on July 19."

To my shock, my birth certificate stated a baby girl named Sandra/Karen was born on July 18. The name Sandra had been crossed out. I'd always celebrated my birthday on July 19!

Confused and needing clarification, I called Mom. "Do you remember my birth date? Record it in a Bible?" She had not.

With two different dates, I checked out a third source: St. Olaf Lutheran Church where I was baptized. The church's certificate listed my birthday as July 17. With three different dates of July 17, 18, and 19, I sought one more proof of my real birthday, the *Turtle Lake Journal*. The newspaper reported a baby girl born to Mr. and Mrs. Albert Schmidt on the 18 of July, the same date as my birth certificate.

The Lord knows my birthday. Until He clarifies it, I insist on celebrating the 17th, 18th, and 19th— just to be sure.

On-the-Job Training

In 1967, a pregnant woman working at National Car Rental in Bismarck, North Dakota, walked off her job. I answered the ad in the paper. Howard hired me. My first day of work, we met at the airport car rental booth. Howard owned the car dealership, which held the National Car Rental license.

"There should be a manual in the desk telling you how to handle rental transactions. Sorry, I don't know anything about the business, never rented a car," he said.

Walking away he added, "We are the only car rental company giving S & H Green Stamps. You will find the dispenser and an extra roll of stamps in the far right drawer."

I caught on fast—you don't rent cars to people without credit cards.

I Can't Live Without You

When Cam and Del were in grade school, Delmer and I lived in Bismarck. On Tuesday nights, I bowled with a women's league. My babysitter called me at the bowling alley.

"Your husband stormed out of the house yelling, 'Someone's going to pay,' and drove away." He traveled as a service man; I didn't know he was back in town.

Running out of the bowling alley, I hurried home, paid the babysitter, and said, "Leave in case things turn violent. I'll be OK, don't worry."

Shortly after the babysitter left, my husband's truck pulled into our driveway. My heart pounded wildly. I focused my attention on our front door as Delmer walked into the house.

"Are you having an affair with Pat? I can't live without you," he shouted. His eyes glared at me. He meant business.

Pat owned a local bar. My girlfriend, Nicky, and I hung out at Pat's bar. We played pool, danced to the juke box, drank screwdrivers, and told funny stories.

Nicole, an attractive redhead from France, wounded many a man's heart. Men hung on her French accent and all her words. Nicky lived across the street from us, so we exchanged babysitting. Her daughter, Carol Ann, and Cam were the same age.

Party life with Nicky, wow, I had never experienced such freedom. Drinking made me feel taller, smarter, and cuter.

Growing up, Lou and Gay bought one bottle of Mogen David wine at Thanksgiving. The children were allowed a small glass. Other than that no alcohol was ever in our house.

Pat's winning smile, black hair, brown eyes, and slim body turned every woman's head. More importantly, he paid attention to me. I soaked up his affection like a sponge. After that night—no more party girl for me. No bars without my husband. But I did drink alone at home.

***

One day while working at the Bismarck National Car Rental counter, I watched as the people disembarked from the plane. I saw an old familiar smile: Pat. I hadn't seen him in over a year. Patrick picked up his suitcase, and then stopped by my booth.

"Come on, let's have a cup of coffee at the airport café," he said.

"I don't know where to start," Pat said looking down. "It's been so long since we've seen each other. I've left my wife." Lifting his head our eyes met. The fun-loving glow, gone; his eyes dull, not a spark.

My coffee turned cold as Pat confessed, "I'm in love for the first time in my life. I've found the perfect 'partner.' I won't be moving back to Bismarck."

Our friendship now made sense. We always enjoyed each other's company but were never physically intimate.

North Dakota to Minnesota

Delmer moved from North Dakota to Minnesota for his job. The boys and I followed. Things between us didn't improve. We never fought, but we weren't able to communicate. We divorced—agreeing that the distance between us seemed too great for reconciliation.

The only thing he said at our meeting with the counselor, "I should not have left you alone so much."

I'd seen some of my friends go through divorces, and most of them didn't seem to suffer—but I was deeply grieved and hurt.

I sold my piano and bought my son, Del, a silver trumpet. The rest of the money from selling the piano went for the expense of the moving truck. Only the boys' bedroom sets, toys, clothes, and my personal things were loaded for the trip back to North Dakota.

House, furniture, savings accounts, and combined acquired assets of our fourteen-year marriage were left for Delmer. I didn't ask him for one penny of alimony.

With Tammy Wynette singing, "D-I-V-O-R-C-E becomes final today and me and little J-O-E are moving away," Del, Cam, and I headed out of Minneapolis in our dark blue Pontiac Bonneville.

Minnesota to North Dakota

The move back to North Dakota was not well received by my relatives. They loved Delmer. I did too. It just turned out we were totally opposite. I was looking for something I had never received from another adult—love.

My sons' love for me and mine for them was definitely unconditional. We thought of ourselves as the three musketeers. I told them, "You can do anything you want in life with God, education, and love."

Before moving, I'd lined up a job as manager of the Minot National Car Rental airport office. It seemed I couldn't get away from the car rental business. My sons were old enough to help me clean cars on weekends and get them ready for the next week.

I faced yet another loss when I returned to Minot. Downriver from where I rented a home for the boys and I, sat my brother Russell's house. He graduated from high school before I started, so I never really knew him and I would never get the chance.

Late one night a year ago, Russell was driving home to Minot from Turtle Lake. A drunk driver crashed into my brother's Volvo, killing him instantly. It was near the town of Velva and close to where my father had also died in a car accident. Russell left behind two small sons and his grieving wife, Twilla.

* * *

Many times after my divorce, I was free to fly on my own, but I crashed more than once—looking for someone, anyone, to love me.

I drank a lot of vodka and developed a "come here, go away" personality. This made me feel safe. I could abandon a man before he abandoned me.

Hope for the Dark Days

Before I formed you in the womb I knew you,

before you were born I set you apart.

Jeremiah 1:5 NIV

"Learn to be wise," he said, "and develop

good judgment and common sense!

I cannot overemphasize this point."

Cling to wisdom—and she will protect you.

Love her—she will guard you.

Getting wisdom is the most important

thing you can do!

Proverbs 4:5-6 TLB

Do not be afraid nor dismayed...

for the battle is not yours, but God's.

2 Chronicles 20:15 TLB

Me at the National Car Rental booth in the Bismarck
Airport. Hot pants and boots were all the rage.

~ 5 ~

Rocky Mountain High

North Dakota to Colorado Springs 1977

*A*nthony was a tall Italian with curly, coal black hair—and a master's degree. I've always admired people with college degrees. His degree could have been storytelling. Fact or fiction, he wove spellbinding words together. We became lovers.

When Honeywell hired him to work in Colorado Springs, he asked, "Would you consider moving with me?" On one knee, he added, "Marry me."

Head over heels in love, I moved with my two sons from Minot to Teeter Totter Circle in the shadow of Pikes Peak. Little did I realize our house on Teeter Totter would live up to its name.

My second day in town, I drove out to National Car Rental at the Colorado Springs airport and applied for a job. They needed a night manager and I qualified. I needed to know I'd be able to provide for my sons, just in case. Getting another job wasn't a problem; I'd developed a strong work ethic as a young girl on the farm.

Funny how these memories come back to me now. Always trying hard to be a good girl, I'd clean the gutters of the barn in the mornings before riding my horse to school. Uncle Gay gave me a cow which I cared for in the evening. During my senior year, I sold my cow's calf in order to buy my senior class ring. But I'd also earned enough money to buy a Samsonite suitcase and pay for six months of business college. Thankfully, even though it was a lot of hard work, I enjoyed working on the farm, all of the animals, and the fresh air.

Sunny mornings and then dark nights played out like a movie of passion and deceit. I found bottles of whiskey stashed all over the house. Six months after my move, I became the sole bread winner. After a year, I had no illusions or hope that the situation would improve.

As the house on Teeter Totter started tottering up and down, it jarred my innermost being. On the shelf in my bedroom with all the books stood a very different book. When opened, you'd see a hiding place to save money for a rainy day. The anticipated rainy day occurred on a windy fall day.

While the boys were in school and Anthony on the golf course, I hired a moving truck. I took my stuff, the boys stuff, and left his stuff—including his wet bar. We went into hiding in a condo on the other side of town.

Thank you, Jesus, for finding me a refuge away from verbal and physical abuse. No stale booze odor in our home.

Two weeks later, our quiet was shattered. Anthony had followed one of my sons home from school. Knocking at the door, Anthony said, "I want a second chance. Why did you leave me? I love you. I'm sorry. Move back."

"No!" I replied.

He grabbed me. My blouse tore. The boys and I fled to the safety of a motel. Days later, I called my neighbor. They told me Anthony left my condo escorted by the police.

Walking into my home, it was hard to comprehend the destruction: broken whiskey bottles on the floor; brown stains on the carpet; telephone ripped from the wall and used as a hammer; pieces of glass from broken picture frames shattered on my bed; dots of his blood spattered on the walls; plants overturned and left wilting, dying; jewelry ripped apart; treasured heirlooms gone.

"We called the police because of all the racket," my neighbor said.

My past grief and heartaches had always been my responsibility. I kept my private life to myself. A gnawing gut feeling told me: *Call Uncle Gay and Aunt Lou in North Dakota.* They were now in their golden years.

Hearing my voice, they started crying. They asked, "Are you all right? Anthony called and told us you were kidnapped and placed in a prostitution ring in Chicago."

I found out he also called my ex-husband to tell him the same lie.

* * *

The boys and I loved Colorado Springs. Cameron excelled at football and basketball. His height topping six-feet, four-inches helped. Del played his silver trumpet, first chair in the high school jazz band. Del also placed first at swim meets for his strong breast stroke. Snow-capped mountains with ski lifts were another selling point. However, we had no relatives or personal friends living in Colorado. The three of us voted, "Yes, stay—no to moving."

"My dream is to graduate from high school and then attend the Air Force Academy in Colorado Springs," Del said.

* * *

"I mean it! Send Happy Winston to me," Anthony said, his voice sounding a long way from Colorado Springs.

My birthday present from him, two years prior, had been an English bulldog, Happy Winston of Black Forest. Happy Winston and I spent our last night together curled up on the sofa. As I drove her to the airport the next morning, Happy Winston pushed her already flat face against the passenger's window. Drivers smiled and pointed at her. This little dog really loved me and now she was leaving. My emotions sunk to a new low. I never saw Happy Winston again, nor did I hear from Anthony.

Out of the Frying Pan into the Fire 1980

My dating life had been non-existent for the last year. All the destruction Anthony caused, as he wreaked havoc in my life, stripped away my strength. Arranging a moving truck for the second time and leaving Anthony, who I thought I loved, was one of the hardest jobs on earth. My only release was crying.

The romantic part of my broken-heart screamed: *What's wrong with me? What man is ever going to love me? I have no value!*

The fourth of July found me alone. Del and Cam were visiting their father for a couple of months. I always managed to get into trouble when the boys were gone for the summer. The freedom of being able to stay out late or even all night was hard for me to fathom.

"What are you doing the night of the fourth?" my neighbor Mary asked.

"Just staying home, reading, and cleaning, nothing exciting."

"Come over. I've invited a few friends for a barbeque. Watching fireworks will be fun," my friend said.

It was a hot night, at least by Colorado Springs standards, perfect night for a pale blue sun dress.

I arrived at Mary's, adding my salad to the party food, and poured myself a drink.

A handsome man with salt and pepper hair and broad shoulders appeared at the screen door. His dark brown eyes were set off with thick black eyebrows. He looked like a retired professional football player who was still very much in shape.

"Hi, I'm Richard," he said, sitting down next to me with his drink in hand.

Two weeks later on my July 18 birthday, Richard proposed to me. Getting down on one knee he asked, "Will you marry me?" He handed me a box with a necklace, my ruby birthstone in the shape of a heart. Diamonds encircled the heart.

"Yes," I answered. Richard placed the necklace around my neck and hooked the 18-karat-gold clasp.

My relationships had always begun with a strong physical attraction. *This must be the one. I'm going to be married. Richard told me he loved me.*

* * *

On our wedding trip to Las Vegas, I discovered Richard loved to play cards. By the second night in Vegas, I was exhausted and had no strength left to stand by the blackjack table to watch. Two hundred dollars up, five hundred dollars down, up, down, no way could anyone keep track. Finding an oversized chair in the lounge, I curled up and fell asleep.

Some hours later Richard woke me up and I learned the blackjack dealers had all our money. Eventually, even my high school graduation ring was pawned for the game.

Colorado Springs to San Diego

A few months into our marriage, Richard said, "I've got a friend in San Diego. Duane and his wife said I could stay with them. Lots of money to be made in California, I'm heading west to try my luck. Want to move?"

"No, I have to stay in Colorado Springs for at least one more year. Remember? Del's seeking an appointment to the Academy."

Richard moved to San Diego; the boys and I stayed in Colorado.

After Del's acceptance into the Academy, Cam and I moved to San Diego. Richard had changed over the last year of living by himself in San Diego. Of course, what did I know about him?

The second week after moving to San Diego I landed a job at Budget Car Rental. In a short time, I worked my way up to manager, opening new car rental offices all over San Diego County. The job, as usual, came with benefits, including a company car and gas.

After two short years in California, Richard said, "Kc, the insurance market in Denver seems better. I'm going back, staying with my boss and his wife. There's lots of money to be made in Colorado."

Richard came back to San Diego for a visit after his first month in Colorado.

"Let's go out for dinner tonight and walk on the beach," I said, "haven't seen you in weeks."

Walking on the beach back to the oceanfront furnished condo Cam and I rented, Richard said, "I'm going back to Denver tomorrow. Are you sure you don't want to move back?" Windblown waves roared, drowning out his voice.

A friend in Denver told me, "I think you need to come to

Colorado, or be prepared to say good-bye to your husband." The implication was anything but subtle.

I didn't bring up the subject of infidelity. *How could he love me and act like that?* Doubting Richard's love, this time I didn't follow my man.

"When are you coming back?" I said as we shared a cup of espresso the next morning. The ocean mist dampened our last kiss, he didn't answer my question.

I worked late knowing Richard had left for Colorado and Cameron was at football practice. I was shocked when I got home. Richard's clothes and personal things were all gone, cleared out, everything but his dirty shorts in the laundry basket.

Standing on the balcony, I stared at the ocean, overcome by loneliness. *He deserted me. How could my husband leave without an explanation? "Lord, what's wrong with me? Why can't someone love me … love me?"*

When Cameron arrived home, I told him what happened. "What should we do? We don't know anyone in California. Do you want to stay or move back to Colorado Springs or North Dakota? We don't need to worry about money, my job's good, always nice cars to drive." A definite perk of being in the rental car business were the flashy, fast convertibles to drive, free gas, and no car insurance to worry about.

"Mom, I love it here. Let's stay in San Diego. Del can come home from the Academy on breaks and surf with me. We don't need anyone, Mom, we're fine, just you and me."

The divorce papers arrived in Denver just in time for Richard to sign before he took off to the east coast. He took all our money, bought a new sports car, and I never heard from him again.

Hope for the Dark Days

My eyes are ever looking to the Lord for help,

for He alone can rescue me. Come Lord,

and show me your mercy, for I am helpless,

overwhelmed, in deep distress; my problems

go from bad to worse. Oh, save me from them all!

See my sorrows; feel my pain; forgive my sins.

Psalm 25:15-18 TLB

Yes, the Lord hears the good man

when he calls to him for help,

and saves him out of all his troubles.

Psalm 34:17 TLB

~ 6 ~

Lou, Like a Mother

I always thought of Louise as my mother figure—
with her big brown eyes and hair black as the raven.
She was happiest when cooking and canning in the
kitchen. Louise's baking made her the star of the Lutheran
Ladies Aid. For every church meeting, she prepared cake,
pie, cupcakes, or a special meatloaf.

Trees were dropping their leaves in preparation for
a cold, white winter. Thanksgiving was around the corner.
Louise's seventy-second birthday, November 25, a double
celebration. Louise loved this season of the year. The
smell of turkey and dressing would fill the house. The lace
tablecloth, silverware, and china hidden away in the old
cupboard would be brought out to use again.

No entertaining this year, 1979, Louise was weak
and tired. She had found a lump in her stomach. The doctor
operated and removed a cancerous tumor the size of a small
melon. After radiation and chemo treatments, Louise's body
seemed to be healing.

In the Name of Jesus 1982

Later at the age of seventy-five, Louise developed an infection. Dr. Kuplis, Turtle Lake's doctor, thought Trinity Hospital in Bismarck was the best place for Lou. My plane from San Diego arrived in Bismarck at 1:00 p.m.

"Gay, have you done any fishing this year?" I asked, as we sat in Lou's hospital room.

"No, guess my body's slowing down. I've sold my boat," he replied. We visited for a couple hours. "Since you're staying here with Louise tonight, my sister wants me to sleep at her place in Mandan."

"I'll see you in the morning, goodnight, I love you," I said, as Gay left the hospital with his sister.

Louise started tossing and turning in bed about 6:00 p.m. She tried crawling out of bed and pulled the covers over her head. I kissed her cheek and propped pillows around her to try and make her more comfortable.

"God is here with us, my sweet Louise. Try and rest. Gay will be back in the morning."

She could not settle down. The temperature in her room dropped. The air became colder, I struggled to breathe. *Is this the calm before the storm? Are my instincts correct? Death, are you drawing near to my precious Louise?* Deep in thought, I paced the floor. A nurse walked into Lou's room.

"Louise seems restless and now doesn't respond to my voice. Is she dying?" I asked.

"No, she's fine. I check her vitals every half hour," the nurse answered.

It felt as if a superhuman evil force had crept into the dark hospital room. My body and mind could not handle this evil. I clutched my Bible close to my chest.

Louise woke up and wanted a drink of water. After drinking the water, her body started shaking. Worried, I stroked her hair. The room got colder; my senses heightened. Nurses quietly entered and left her room while making their rounds.

I remembered something my cousin Kearney, a Lutheran minister, said: "Karen, if you feel afraid or sense Satan's presence, call on the Lord." I kept those words close.

Around 3:00 a.m. Louise twisted in bed, looking uncomfortable. Leaning over her, I repeated The Lord's Prayer. Next I recited Psalm 23: *"The Lord is my Shepherd, I shall not want. He makes me to lie down in green pastu..."*

Wham! A hand slapped me hard across the face. I staggered backwards. *Who? What?*

My eyes opened twelve inches away from a horrible, gruesome face. I'd never seen this face before: big black terrifying eyes, a demonic look as her face twisted out of shape, the smile all teeth and no lips.

Suddenly, realizing this must be the agent of temptation, I said, "Satan, be gone in the name of Jesus! Louise is a child of the King and you can't have her. She's going home." I bawled.

Louise's body relaxed in bed. She slowly opened her brown eyes and smiled peacefully. She didn't speak but took a couple deep breaths, turned on her side, and snored.

Tonight was frightening and confusing as I knew I'd come face-to-face with the chief of fallen angels.

Stroking her hair with my fingertips, I sensed death closing in. Running to the nurse's station I called, "Louise is dying, hurry."

"Call a doctor," yelled a nurse checking her vitals. "Mrs. Kalland's kidneys have failed."

When the doctor arrived, he said, "Call the family."

Uncle Gerhard received my call in the early morning light, "Better come to the hospital," I said. Louise had been his bride for forty-two years.

A couple years earlier, my pastor told me, "When you die, someone you love will come to usher you into heaven."

Louise's room turned warm. Her long thin arm lifted, her finger pointed to the ceiling's north corner. She spoke quietly, barely audible, "Al, Albert."

I believe Louise saw my dad, her brother, and God coming to usher her home to heaven.

Hope for the Dark Days

Be careful—watch out for attacks from Satan,

your great enemy. He prowls around like

a hungry, roaring lion, looking for some victim

to tear apart. Stand firm when he attacks.

Trust the Lord; and remember that other

Christians all around the world are

going through these sufferings too.

1 Peter 5:8–9 TLB

His loved ones are very precious to him

and he does not lightly let them die.

Psalm 116:15 TLB

I will trust in you and not be afraid, for the Lord

is my strength and song; he is my salvation.

Isaiah 12:2 TLB

Aunt Louise and Uncle Gerhard

~ 7 ~

Crazy Alone 1983

Richard left our marriage. Both of my sons were at the Air Force Academy. I'd been promoted at work and needed to move to Laguna Beach. Worries moved in and wouldn't let me sleep without the help of pills—and a vodka bottle.

One night I drove to my favorite bar on the beach for happy hour. One, two, three, four vodka martinis with olives—I felt very happy. Unable to drive, I walked home on the sandy beach. Happiness faded as I sobered.

Someone help me; make this hurt go away. I'm so lonesome. Miss my sons.

Sleep eluded me. Just one more drink with orange juice to make it healthy, then a couple of Tylenol PM. Oh, to sleep peacefully for one night.

The telephone rang. I couldn't answer. I turned in bed and saw the clock hands pointing straight up: noon. Staggering to the bathroom, my pounding head and shaking body screamed: Sick day! Yesterday's clothes, pressed to my body, were fine for my day at home. I planned the day: a small drink, a nap, a cocktail, and watch the sunset.

With a busy work schedule, I never found time to form friendships and I had no one to talk to about my demons. I needed professional help.

Growing up in North Dakota, we assumed only people who were nuts saw a psychiatrist. Crazy people were the ones who waved their hands uncontrollably or screamed all the time, we thought. No one in my family had been to a psychiatrist.

My relatives lived far away and wouldn't find out how desperate my life had become. Slowly, I dialed a number from the yellow pages.

I don't remember the psychiatrist's face. He sat behind a big desk; I wiggled on a very small chair.

"Why are you here?" he asked coldly.

"I don't know, I'm crying, just crying all the time. No one loves me." Tears rolled down my cheeks.

"There are many reasons people come to me for help," the psychiatrist stated matter-of-factly. He listed a few of them, and added, "Tell me if you have *one* of these problems."

"No wonder I'm here! Nine of the things you just mentioned have happened to me. Not just one, but all nine." I rattled on.

The doctor seemed to be listening and wrote something down on his note pad. It satisfied me. I talked, he listened.

1. Divorce—Second husband moved out.

2. Death of a parent—Louise raised me, she died of cancer. Dad was killed in car accident.

3. Death of a sibling—Russell killed by a drunk driver.

4. Job—Big promotion at Budget Car Rental.

5. Change of home—I'd given up my cozy beach condo.

6. Moving to a new city—Plans to move to Laguna Beach.

7. Empty Nest—Sons at the Air Force Academy in Colorado Springs. I'd never lived by myself—scary. The boys loved me, but right now their careers came first, not mom.

8. Money—Ex-husband left me with all his debts.

9. Health—Booze-happy. Pills-sleep. Another recently discovered lump in my breast would have to wait for a biopsy. The first one tested was not malignant; I didn't have time to worry about this one.

I didn't go back to the psychiatrist. He'd placed structure around the nine categories of why my life sucked. The only thing I remember, the psychiatrist telling me, "Richard, is a flim-flam man. He goes from one person to another getting what he can, never giving anything back."

Like everything else, I would try working through this alone. "Deal with it!" That's how I was brought up.

Oh, Lord, how can I hang on? There are so many cards stacked against me; my life and body are crumbling. Can you mend my broken heart?

I Forgot How Much You Love Me

When I returned home, I saw my uncle's worn, dusty *The Living Bible* on the shelf. This translation was easier to understand than the *King James Bible*. Many years ago the Bible had been my good friend—but lately I'd been chasing wild dreams, or chasing dreams wildly.

Clutching the Bible to my chest, years of pent-up pain flooded onto the pages. Tears fell as I knelt and prayed with the Psalmist: *"But Lord, you are my shield, my glory, and my only hope. You alone can lift my head, now bowed in shame"* (Psalm 3:3 TLB).

"I've made such a mess of my life doing it my way. I forgot how much You love me. Forgive me," I prayed.

Over the next few months, I read *The Living Bible* from cover to cover. My courage, faith, and trust in God were slowly reborn.

For as long as I could remember, I'd lived in fear of not being loved. I tried so hard to be the best I could be. But it never seemed to be enough to please: my parents, aunt, uncle, two husbands, or lover. I'd replaced my lack of security with my ability to work hard, earn a good living, keep my boys safe, and make them feel the unconditional love I never knew.

My new faith of trusting Jesus assured me that someone loved me! I'd forgotten He loved me so much He died on the cross for me. Unlike worldly love, God's love is unconditional. Looking for love with the opposite sex had almost proven fatal.

When fingers wrapped around my neck as a man tried to choke me, Jesus was there. The black and blue finger marks on my throat were covered with scarves for weeks.

Jesus also rescued me when another man gave me a black eye. These cases could have been worse but Jesus protected me. He lifted me out of one grotesque nightmare after another and placed my feet on solid ground. Jesus loved me just as I was. The Holy Spirit entered my life and started teaching me wisdom. *My sins were forgiven!*

Hope for the Dark Days

"I lay down and slept in peace and woke up safely,

for the Lord was watching over me."

Psalm 3:5 TLB

But he knows every detail of what

is happening to me.

Job 23:10 TLB

~ 8 ~

California Soul Mate 1984

The Comedy Store in LaJolla is advertising top comedians, I'll drive and even pay. Let's get out tonight," Patti said, as we sat chatting in the hot tub. We both lived at See the Sea, in separate condo units, directly in front of the Crystal Pier in Pacific Beach.

Driving by The Comedy Store, Patti said, "The line of people waiting to get in goes around the block. No way I'm standing in that line."

"Don't feel like going home. The Catamaran Hotel's ad said they are having a great band. That's close to home. If we drink too much, we'll walk home on the beach," I responded.

We walked into the Catamaran and found a booth close to the band.

Vodka was still my friend. I ordered a martini.

"Do you want to dance?" I looked up into a young man's face.

"No thanks. Just want to listen to the music." He was cute, but I wasn't looking for, nor interested in another quick, heart-breaking relationship.

"Great band. Guy, the guitarist, is married to my cousin," the man said.

"Good song, I'll dance with you," Patti said.

As I sat alone at the table, I thought, *that's the last thing I want ... a man. Three times ... enough!*

When Patti and her dance partner returned from the dance floor, she slid into the booth and he sat down next to her.

"Jerry, my name's Jerry Hutter," he told us. He turned out to be a talker, full of unbelievable stories about scuba diving for treasure. We laughed and drank. When the band was on a break, Jerry introduced us to his cousin, Lynette, Guy's wife.

"What's your phone number, Kc?" Jerry asked, as we were getting ready to leave.

"Phone number? I'm not in the dating mode right now and you're too young."

He whipped out his wallet. Patti checked his driver's license. "Kc, he's only two years younger than you."

He looks twenty years younger. Maybe the sea salt pickled his face, I thought.

I didn't give him my number. Jerry walked us to my car. He handed me his Florida business card with his mother's telephone number in San Diego written on the back. He had just moved back from Florida. After opening my car door, his lips gently touched mine. "Goodnight," he said.

During our conversation, he heard me talk about Budget Car Rental. Over the next couple of weeks he called Budget, but no one knew Kc. It turned out Jerry called Budget at the airport. I worked for Budget San Diego County.

Listening to "Flash Dance" on my cassette player, I'd do my daily run on the beach. My body and mind were getting ready for the big move to Laguna Beach. Reading my Bible each day was also a part of my routine.

A few weeks passed. One day when I reached into my purse, Jerry's card fell out. "Call him," a small voice said.

Oh yea, Lord, just what I need! A man who boasts of sea treasure diving trips, drives a classic primer grey 53 Chevy surf van, has no job, and lives with his mother.

As more time went by, the little voice again said, "Call Jerry."

Finally, I picked up the phone, "Is Jerry there, please?"

A woman answered. I assumed she was his mother. "No, he's not. May I take a message?"

"This is Kc. I met Jerry a few months ago."

"Kc, Jerry told me about you. Please leave your number. He's been trying to find you. I'm Ruth, Jerry's mom."

The next day, Jerry called and asked me for a date. "I'm so thankful you called. I couldn't get you out of my mind. I have walked Pacific Beach many evenings hoping I'd see you."

We met—again at the Catamaran—flowers on the table. I listened; he talked. He was a college graduate and a CPA. He had been divorced three times and had two grown sons. He'd lived on his sailboat in the Caribbean islands for three years, was a boat builder, sign company owner, adventurer, surfer, and treasure diver.

I Fall for You 1984

What an exciting time in my life—moving up the coast, assistant to the president of a large car rental company. Top of the ladder at last.

Friday morning, I scouted out two places to rent in Laguna Beach. First choice, a house on the beach; second choice, an artist's cottage with a view of the ocean, a loft, baby grand piano, and carrousel horse.

I jumped into my red Mustang convertible and pushed a button rolling the top back. The wind styled my hair on the drive to San Diego. Tonight, I had a date with Jerry.

Wanting to impress him, I dressed in leather pants, matching leather jacket, and high heeled boots. My long false nails needed a quick paint job, bright red—perfect.

The topic of our dinner conversation revolved around the high surf crashing on our favorite beach, Windansea, in La Jolla. We were always amazed at how waves rearranged the beach scenery. Within a few days, the waves could remove all the sand, exposing fingers of steep craggy rocks extending into the ocean.

We decided to check out the high surf. Sightseers lined the coastal road watching the storm. Waves crashed on the rocks to over twenty feet in the air. The night sky, darkest black, no moon or stars. Waves flung seaweed. A salty odor filled the air. Each wave of ocean spray stung our faces. We walked holding hands, trying to avoid the deep channels. Turning around, we started back to Jerry's van. A deafening wave slammed over the rocks, stopping us to admire the force of the sea.

Jerry turned to the right and walked behind the beach fire some people had built.

I stepped forward. "Help!" I screamed. My body fell into a fifteen foot crevice. Landing on my bottom on a large rock, my butt failed to cushion the fall.

"Kc—Kc!" Jerry yelled. He jumped into the crevice, grabbed me, and pulled me to safety just before a wave would have taken me out to sea.

"My Hero!"

The people around the fire saw me fall. Their fire had temporarily blinded me. They called out, "Lady, you want a beer?"

"No thanks!" I hollered back.

"Jerry, this pain is worse than childbirth. I've pulled a muscle," I said. Even in pain I was vain. Looking carefully at my hands, I said, "Look, no broken fingernails."

Jerry helped me to the bed in the back of his van and gave me several Tylenol. The pain would not go away.

"Jerry, take me to the hospital emergency room," I said, after a couple hours.

After X-rays, the doctor came in, "You have not pulled a muscle. You have broken your back."

The Lord's plan for my life is not Laguna Beach: U-turn.

After being in the hospital fourteen days, I was ready to be released. A chaplain came in to pray with me. The telephone rang as the chaplain said, "Amen."

Lord, what now? I'm flat on my back and in a body brace. What about my job? I've already moved out of my San Diego home. No relatives or friends to call for help. I don't want to worry my sons at the Air Force Academy.

Broken Back 1984

"Kc, I have an extra room in my home. I heard about your accident. Come and stay with me," Ruth said.

I thought about it for awhile. I had only met Ruth a couple of times, she seemed nice. But I didn't know if I wanted to be around Jerry with a broken back. I was still trying to impress him. My choices were limited.

"Thanks Ruth, I'll take you up on the offer, but only if I can pay you rent, install a business phone, and meet with my managers at your home until I'm back on my feet."

"Of course, anything you want. But you don't have to pay me. My home is your home," Ruth said.

My back healed. Ruth and I became great friends. Things were getting serious with Jerry. He loved me even with a broken back. Guess I needed to ask him the million dollar question—the deal breaker.

"Jerry, who do you say Jesus is?"

"I had perfect attendance for fourteen years at the Episcopal church. Jesus was a great man," Jerry answered.

"If you don't believe Jesus died for our sins on the cross and *IS* the Son of God, we can never marry," I replied.

Mr. Jerry Lee Hutter, an educated man, often read until four o'clock in the morning.

"Jerry, what star constellation is that? Who served as the twenty-fifth President?" I'd ask. He'd answer.

Deep space astronomy, archeology, opera, jazz, cooking, plants, economics, sailing, surfing, banking, anything—I asked him questions. He knew the answers. Usually, after he'd been talking for fifteen minutes, I'd say, "Honey, this is way more information than I need. Thanks."

"Jerry, have you ever read the Bible?"

"No, can't say I have," Jerry said, "just read a few parts."

"You don't know what the book says unless you've read it from cover to cover. There would be no way of visiting with you about *Sailing Alone Around the World* or *Worlds in Collision* or *The Book of Five Rings* if I hadn't read the book," I added.

"Lord, you are first in my life. I don't want to have sex or live with another man unless he is my husband.

"Kc, let's read the Bible together, out loud," Jerry said.

Reading the Bible, Jerry learned the whole story. We were born-again, baptized, and married.

The Bible told us our future. We were, and still are, a great team. The minister who married us gave us this advice, "If you need more kisses, give more kisses. If you need more hugs, give more hugs." Simple, but it works.

Who would love me now? Jerry and the Lord will love me.

Jerry and I have closeness, familiarity, confidence, and friendship. Over the years, I have met all the people Jerry talked about in his stories. All his treasure diving and sea tales proved to be true. He is my constant companion.

Holding a glass of vodka with a floating olive had always made me feel glamorous. Isn't this what actors do on TV and in movies? At a cocktail party, a happy hour, or visiting a friend, I often heard, "do you want a drink?"

After years of drinking, my stomach would hurt and my head pounded every morning. My heart filled with anguish and sorrow. *What words did I say last night? Did I lose control and embarrass myself?* I wondered.

Many times I tried to quit drinking on my own. All of my attempts failed, even though I knew the pain of having a loved one killed by a drunk driver.

Finally I prayed, "Lord, take the need of alcohol from me, make the taste repulsive."

The Lord heard and answered my prayers.

Jerry's first job after we were married—Business Manager for the San Diego Opera. With only twenty extra dollars a week to spend, Ruth helped our budget by visiting all the thrift stores. With our measurements in hand, she purchased the evening attire for all the big events.

One night at the opera *Barber of Seville,* a women walked up to me, "Mrs. Hutter, your gown and coat are exquisite. Where were they purchased?"

I smiled. "I don't know. My mother-in-law buys most of my clothes on her travels." Not a lie. Ruth traveled all over San Diego County. I don't know at which thrift store she purchased my coat and gown. Shhhhhh! Only Ruth and I knew it cost less than twenty dollars—for both pieces.

The year Jerry and I met, 1984

Hope for the Dark Days

Point out the road I must travel;

I'm all ears, all eyes before you.

Psalm 143:8 The Message

Two can accomplish more than twice as

much as one, for the results can be much

better. If one falls, the other pulls him up; but

if a man falls when he is alone, he's in

trouble. Also, on a cold night, two under the

same blanket gain warmth from each other.

Ecclesiastes 4:9–11 TLB

Who has woe? Who has sorrow? Who has strife?

Who has complaints? Who has needless bruises?

Who has bloodshot eyes? Those who linger over wine, who go to

sample bowls of mixed wine. ... In the end

it bites like a snake and poisons like a viper.

Proverbs 23:29-30, 32 NIV

~ 9 ~

Call on the Name of the Lord

My cousin Kearny lived in Costa Mesa, California, and invited me to lunch one day. We spent the morning making house calls to sick people in his congregation. I heard him remind many people to call on the name of the Lord to be saved, to be free from fear, and to be healed. The assurance of his words worked their way into my thoughts and mind.

Heading my yellow Mustang convertible towards home after our relaxing day, I began thinking about the times I'd faced extreme circumstances in my life. There was no shaking or trembling, I'd simply become frozen in place. I couldn't do anything until I saw what others were going to do.

I remembered the time my sister, LuJean, and I had taken our speedboat out on Long Lake in Minnesota. I was at the helm as we towed our two children behind in a canoe. The canoe crested the wave made by the boat and flipped upside down. Our five-year-old children were dumped into the cold water. Seeing the accident in my rear view mirror, I quickly stopped the boat.

"Help," the children yelled, as they bobbed up and down. They were clearly in danger. But I sat frozen and watched.

"Hurry, turn around! We need to pick them up!" LuJean screamed.

I did and we rescued the frightened kids. But I wondered: *How long would I have just sat and watched?*

Now with Kearney's words "call on the name of the Lord" as my strategy for dealing with fear, I hoped I would respond differently.

Jesus 1990

My business "Sunbelt Car Rental," where we rented Corvette and Mustang convertibles, was located near the San Diego Airport. Our slogan "Fun in the Sun" often brought in customers. On this particular Monday, business was slow. I worked alone on the property, which was quite a distance from any other businesses.

A clean-shaven young man about thirty-years-old walked in wearing a bright colored polo shirt, dress slacks, and carrying a duffel bag with "Padres Baseball" printed on the side.

"I saw your sign. Do you have a Mustang convertible available today?" he asked.

"Yes," I said, "a red Mustang should return in about an hour. Will that work for you?"

"Sure. Mind if I wait?"

"Fine. Have a seat and make yourself comfortable." I took him a glass of water.

I forgot all about the young man sitting with eyes closed in the corner about ten feet from my desk. He had not said another word.

I got back to work checking our reservation book and in about half an hour, I sensed danger. Looking up, I saw a gun pointed directly at me.

"Don't hurt me!" I managed to get out.

He pulled a chair up-close to the desk blocking any chance of escape. The scary gun was now inches from my heart.

"There's a couple hundred dollars in petty cash. Take any of the cars," I said motioning to the car key board.

Kearney's advice for handling fear rushed through my brain: "If you're ever terrified, call on God."

"Jesus," I said. I don't know if it was soft or a loud shout, but it was all I could get out. Through the corner of my eye, I could see the man's expression explode into fear. *Is my guardian angel or the Lord himself standing behind me?* I wondered.

My assailant tossed the metal chair he had been sitting on across the room, stuffed the gun into his duffel bag, and ran out the front door.

Jumping up, I ran to the door to see which way he was heading. He was running toward my friend's office at Park and Ride. I dialed 911. Then I called Park and Ride to alert them that a man with a gun was coming their way.

The police arrived and searched the area but found no one. An officer dusted the water glass, retrieving fingerprints. I was able to give a good description of him in my report.

Rape? Robbery? I'll never know the stranger's intentions.

Not Yet 1991

"Icky, what a rainy morning," I said to Clay, working at the front desk. "I'm going to the bank."

Usually, I drove my Volvo, but today a small, blue Ford Festiva needed a test drive. The last renter complained about the brakes. I picked up the bank bag and jumped into the roller-skate-sized Festiva.

At the bottom of a steep hill, the railroad crossing barrier arms were coming down; the lights started blinking to warn drivers about an oncoming train. No problem. The Festiva stopped safely. Looking to my left, I saw the Amtrak train speeding down the tracks.

Suddenly, I heard the loud screeching noise of skidding tires on the asphalt. I stared motionless at the scene in my rearview mirror. Sliding down the hill behind me came a truck.

My car is going to be pushed onto the railroad track and crushed by the locomotive. I closed my eyes. The screeching continued. I repeated one word over and over: "Jesus! Jesus!"

All was silent except the steady rhythm of clickity-clack, the lonely clickity-clack of the train and the screech of truck tires and brakes. I sat tensely, anticipating for the crash.

I thought about my life as it passed quickly in front of me. I'd always tried to consider my sons when I made decisions. I wanted the best for them, which included having a relationship with God, traveling the world, getting a college degree, and knowing they were loved.

My goal to witness my sons in their cap and gown at college graduation had been achieved.

In 1985, Del graduated with honors from the Air Force Academy. Cadets tossed their hats and the Thunderbirds flew overhead. What a magnificent Kodak moment! Del fulfilled his dream of becoming a jet pilot.

He told me, "Mom, go see the movie *Top Gun* if you want to know what I do for a living." Now he was flying T-38 jets, and married with two children. I was a grandma.

Cam dislocated his shoulder and couldn't play football for the Air Force Academy. He called me, "Mom, I don't like it here. I'm sitting with my door open in full uniform studying. I want to come back to San Diego."

"Cam, you're throwing away a million dollar education. But you have to follow your dreams. If you come back, promise me you'll get a college degree."

He promised, and came back from Colorado to graduate from San Diego State with a degree in International Business.

I found Jerry, my soul mate. A man who played the guitar and sang love songs to me; who brought not just romance, but the intimacy of two people knowing each other well into my life. He loved me.

Through hard work, I became successful in my career. But I've always been very fearful of the thought of dying.

I opened my eyes as the speeding truck behind me sped by my driver's door. When it stopped, the hood dug under the railroad crossing arm. The stopped position of the truck indicated that if he'd hit the rear-end of my Festiva, I'd have been shoved directly onto the tracks. My driver's-side door would have taken the full impact of the crash as it was hit by the locomotive.

Tears rolled down my cheeks. The wooden arms of the signal went up. I recognized the Lord's voice speaking to my spirit and the silence of my heart, "You were spared. Your work for Me on earth is not yet finished. Listen only to My words, 'I love you!'"

Hope for the Dark Days

Is anyone crying for help? God is listening,

ready to rescue you. If your heart is broken,

you'll find God right there; if you're kicked

in the gut, he'll help you catch your breath.

Psalm 34:17-18 The Message

Even when you are chased by those who seek your life,

you are safe in the care of the Lord your God,

just as though you were safe inside his purse!

1 Samuel 25:29 TLB

In my distress I prayed to the Lord

and he answered me and rescued me.

He is for me! How can I be afraid?

What can mere man do to me?

The Lord is on my side, he will help me.

Psalms 118:5-7 TLB

Cam and Del at the Air Force Academy in Colorado Springs, Colorado.

"The bad man went that way," I told police, minutes after the man pointed his gun at me.

Section Three
Songs from the Fire

~ 10 ~

My Business Partner 1992

spent many years working as General Manager for large national rental agencies before starting my own company. By trial and error and without a college education, I climbed the ladder of the car rental industry, managing car rental offices in North Dakota, Colorado, and California. My salary eventually climbed to over $200,000 a year. I enjoyed the use of my company car, a 401(k), and health insurance. Plus, I had the freedom to open car rental offices, attend seminars and conventions, and be my own boss.

Each morning, I grabbed a cup of coffee on the way to work. Finishing the last sip of coffee at my office, I'd plan the day. Checking rental contracts told me how many cars would return. Reservations told me how many people were coming to rent cars. You just never knew who would walk through the door, which made the car rental business exciting to me.

My friend Priscilla told me, "You're making other people rich. If you ever want to start your own rental company, I'll lend you the money."

The offer from Priscilla went on the back burner. Starting a new company required a business partner knowledgeable in sales and operations and willing to work seven days a week, plus holidays.

Jerry, Cameron, and I were talking one afternoon about Priscilla's offer and a possible idea for a new format in car rentals.

"It takes five years for a new company to start making serious money. At my age, I can't take the pressure of stolen cars and renters getting into accidents," I said.

Cameron listened intently, "I'd love to be in business with you, Mom. Let's call Priscilla."

Cam had finished his college marketing degree and worked the last year at Enterprise Car Rental.

Priscilla loaned us $100,000. We named our business "Dirt Cheap Car Rental" because when we lived in North Dakota everyone would say, "I got a dirt cheap deal" when they only had to pay a low price for something.

We agreed one of us would always be on-site at the office during working hours. Soon, Dirt Cheap was singled out on TV as one of the fastest growing, privately-owned companies in San Diego. *San Diego Business Journal* featured us two years in a row. We opened a second office in Los Angles and trademarked our name, enabling us to expand nationally.

With shingles on the top of my head, anxiety attacks, and change of life, Cameron saw me struggling. "Mom, take the rest of the day off. I'll handle it."

How many mothers get the privilege of working seven years with their grown son?

Cam loved me so much he took on the role of overseer. He never wanted me to worry or stress. He suggested the best car for me to drive and best places to live. He also thought ahead and provided an insurance policy with a savings plan for my retirement.

* * *

For each other's protection, we created a Buy-Sell Agreement funded by life insurance policies. This meant if I died, Jerry would receive $500,000, and Cam 100 percent ownership of our company. If Cameron died, his wife, Susan, would receive the $500,000 and I'd own Dirt Cheap. After two years, we paid back our loan from the investor with interest.

A Season of My Life 1998

The spring of 1998 approached. Semi-retired, I needed only to work six hours a day, instead of my usual twelve or fourteen. Cameron took over the business operations in both San Diego and Los Angeles. My wonderful business partner used wisdom and integrity in dealing with the problems.

"Mom, Susan and I want to take you and Jerry for brunch after church. Some restaurant on the water," Cam said, looking out his office door.

"Ruth always spends Easter Sunday with us. Is it okay if she comes along?" I asked.

"That's fine. We'll meet at your house."

Susan and Cameron were expecting their first baby in October. Jerry and I were very excited.

The week before Easter, Jerry and I sat on the dock in front of our home in Coronado Cays. It was an idyllic April day filled with sunshine. Our only worry was what kind of boat to buy.

"I love sailing. But I know you don't like the wind. Maybe this time we'll get a power boat. Our last sixty-four foot sailboat taught me a lesson: Thou shall not covet thy neighbor's large anything," Jerry said, laughing.

"Does life get any better than this?" I added.

Jerry left for work. I took our small dingy out on the water. Sun soaked into every pore. I sipped morning coffee. Relaxing, I pulled the cell phone out of my pocket.

"Marlene, do you have time for a Nordstrom trip? Pick up new lipstick?" I asked. Not a care in the world, another perfect day in San Diego.

* * *

While driving the tractor as a kid, I made a wish list. I'd finally been able to accomplish nearly all of my goals: God in my life; married to a man crazy about me; children well-adjusted in society; living in California; driving a sports car; living on the water; and finally, Christmas spent in my own home.

When I was young, Christmas with Lou and Gay pulled me in many directions. They told me, "Karen, you better not leave us and go see Dorothy and your brothers and sister, we will be too lonesome."

I could hardly wait for Jerry, Del and Beth, Cam and Susan, and all my grandchildren, to be under my roof for the holidays. Christmas presents would be stacked higher than the tree, the fireplace glowing, and a turkey roasting. This would be the best Christmas ever.

Seven Days

On Sunday, May 3, Susan called, "I'm a little worried about Cam. He had a teeth cleaning on Friday and his gums won't stop bleeding."

"Susan, don't worry, maybe Cam is anemic. He just needs some iron," I said, not at all concerned. "Cam's strong. He has never been sick with anything serious."

Cameron went to work on Monday, which happened to be my day off. In the afternoon, he drove to a clinic and had blood work done.

On May 5, Day 1, Tuesday: Susan called, "The doctor wants more blood work on Cam. I'm driving him to the hospital."

On May 6, Day 2, Wednesday: Cam was told he had acute leukemia. Walking into Cam's hospital room, I said, "Hi, how you feeling?"

Cam and Susan were both lying on his small hospital bed. Instead of picking out baby names, they were studying charts about his recovery.

The doctor would not allow flowers in Cam's room. His body contained no white blood cells or platelets. White blood cells attack germs or infection and are always on the lookout for disease. After an injury, colorless platelets gather at the site of the wound and form a threadlike structure to trap blood cells. This forms a clot.

"Sure hope the doc lets me out of here on Saturday. Porsche racing season starts, first race," Cam said.

Susan and I looked at each other. We both forced a smile.

Just then the doctor stepped into the room. "No problem, you're young, only thirty-two years old. Your recovery rate is 70 percent. By your birthday in September, you will be cancer free," the doctor said.

Lord, oh Lord, I know You are here with us. Cam needs to hold his baby. Susan and I love him and want to spend our lives with him. Hear my prayers!

I called everyone on my prayer chain list, and my prayer partner, Barbara. "Pray, pray for Cameron."

I called Horizon Christian Fellowship and asked, "Can one of the pastors go and visit my son in the hospital? Cameron's diagnosis is acute leukemia."

"Sure, Pastor Miles can see Cameron tomorrow," the secretary said.

On May 7, Day 3, Thursday: I met Pastor Miles in the hospital hallway. He was just leaving Cam's room and said, "Cameron is on the fence, could go either way, heaven or hell."

"Mom!" Cam said as I walked into his room. "I know the Lord and believe in Jesus." Tears rolled down his cheeks.

"I know you do my darling," crying right along with him.

We sat and talked in the afternoon. "Look, Cam, there on your windowsill," I said, pointing at two white doves. They cooed.

"Mom, the clock on my desk doesn't work. Would you pick up a couple batteries for it? The order for a truck-load of new cars will have to wait a few days until I get out of here."

"Don't worry. Things are running smoothly at the office. I'll pick up batteries. See you tomorrow. I love you!"

On May 8, Day 4, Friday: Cam got a ride, but not in his Porsche. He was taken by ambulance from the Grossmont Hospital to Scripps Green Hospital. Susan had medical connections and found the best doctors to help Cam beat the leukemia.

On May 9, Day 5, Saturday: "Wow, nice room, Cam. Bet you wish you were out on the golf course," I said. Cameron's window overlooked the Torrey Pines Golf Course in LaJolla.

"I have my clubs in the trunk of the car," Jerry added with a chuckle.

Cam was in a good mood. "Mother's Day is tomorrow. Please pick up something nice for Susan for me. I'd like to surprise her."

"Sure, I'll pick up a couple cute maternity blouses for her. See you tomorrow, love you."

Jerry and I walked to our car.

On May 10, Day 6, Sunday: I called Ruth. "Jerry and I are going to Scripps to see Cam and Susan. Want to ride along?"

When we walked into Cam's room, beside his bed sat a large cardboard box. "Happy Mother's Day," Cam said. "You will love what's in the box."

"Thank you very much. Wow, pretty, and something I can use." I said. Jerry lifted a large white dolphin, holding a round ball for a patio light, from the box.

As we were leaving, Cameron's blue eyes, and my blue eyes blinked a goodbye. It would be the last time here on earth I would ever see his eyes.

"Bye, see you later, get some rest, and don't worry about the office. Love you," I said.

On May 11, Day 7, Monday: "Watch the office for me, Ed. I'm going to the hospital. Something is wrong with Cam."

Driving to Scripps Hospital, I talked with God. *"Lord, I am on my way. What's wrong with Cam? Why tell me to drop everything and go to Cam? Lord, calm my anxious thoughts. Make this feeling of dread disappear."*

I felt an unsettling silence as I walked into Cam's room. That morning I'd typed from memory one of my favorite Bible passages (Jeremiah 29:11) and brought it along for Cam's nightstand: *For I know the plans I have for you. Plans to prosper you not to harm you, plans to give you hope and a future.*

"I love you, Cam. Mom's here. What's wrong baby?" His left eye was swollen and black and blue. He did not respond to my voice. I found the doctor on duty in the hallway.

"What's wrong with Cameron Christman? I tried talking to him and he does not answer. I'm his mother."

"Nothing is wrong. He was a little restless so we gave him a sedative," the doctor told me. "Don't worry; he will be okay."

Walking quickly back to his room, I stood close to the bed. He started to rub his black and blue eye. Reaching for his hand I said, "Don't, honey. Mom is here, the Lord is here, you're going to be all right."

Cam grabbed my hand with all his strength and gave me three strong tugs confirming the three things I'd just said.

This would be my last communication with my beloved son. I ran my fingers through his hair and felt his body cooling. For the second time in my life, I recognized death's fast approaching.

Running into the hall, I screamed, "Get a doctor in here! Help me. My son is dying!"

One, two, three doctors, nurses, the room blurred. They looked under his eyelid with a flashlight, put an oxygen mask over his face, threw the oxygen tank on his bed, and wheeled the bed out of the room.

What just happened? What? What?

* * *

I stood alone in the empty room. Susan and two of her friends arrived. Struggling, I told them what happened. A coldness permeated the atmosphere as the four of us stood looking at each other, holding onto one another. Time stood still.

Finally, the ER doctor stepped into the room. "Call the family. Cameron's brain is hemorrhaging in seven places."

Jerry and I prayed on our knees in the hospital chapel. Our pleas to God went up like incense to the silent expanse above, "Lord, please save Cameron. Lord, let him hold his baby. Cam wants to be a daddy. Oh, Jesus, save his life. His baby needs a father." *Lord, lock shut the doorway to death, please, please.*

I grimaced when walking into the intensive care unit. No doors just shabby-looking drapes shielding others from witnessing the trauma behind them. It seemed as if pain and tears of frustration seeped underneath every curtain.

I felt "the battle of life" raging around me.

My ex-husband Delmer flew in from Iowa. We stood in the darkness by Cam's bed watching as life drained from our son's body. His last breath was suspended ominously between us.

Quiet deathly quiet. Only the hiss, hiss, hiss from the ventilator pumping air into Cam's lungs.

One teardrop hung on Cam's right cheek near his eye. Cam's body made one last movement. Then he lay still. The doctor on duty wheeled the bed away to obtain another brain scan. No one told me. I just knew in my heart his soul had departed.

Lord Jesus, was that the sound of angel wings?

Del, stationed in Germany, was trying to make it to San Diego. At the airport in Texas, he called the hospital. Later, I learned that when he was told Cam had died, he dropped the telephone and fell to the floor sobbing. "Oh no, dear God, I wanted to see my brother one more time."

Del had planned to come back earlier when he heard Cameron had leukemia. Cam told him, "No, this is just a bump in the road. Come back after the baby is born."

The ICU waiting room window ledge had just enough room for me to sit on it. People came and went. My desperate, weary soul was going through the motions of being alive, but inside my spirit felt like it was dying.

"Susan, what do you want to do with Cam's eyes?" Dr. Mason asked the next morning. "His eyes are the only cancer free part of his body."

"We wanted to be organ donors, help other people," Susan said.

"Oh no, Oh no, not his beautiful blue eyes. No, no." I curled into a fetal position, mouthing the words, but making no sound.

Hope for the Dark Days

Where are you God?

The grip on my anchor of faith is slipping.

I'm heading into ultimate loneliness.

* * *

Save me, O my God. The floods have risen.

Deeper and deeper I sink in the mire;

the waters rise around me.

I have wept until I am exhausted;

my throat is dry and hoarse;

my eyes are swollen with weeping,

waiting for my God to act.

Psalm 69:1-3 TLB

"Lord?" My mind closed. The Bible closed. Fog moved in. I still believed in God, but why hadn't He intervened when He is powerful and able? Deep in my heart, I thought maybe Cam was coming back. I could not handle the thought of permanent separation from my child.

Every day I read an inspirational message on a plaque given to me by my friend, Nicole: *"Do not let go of the hope you cherish and confess. Seize it and hold it tight. Put your hope in what I have promised you. For I am reliable, trustworthy, and faithful to my Word."*

* * *

When struggles come and go, we know God strengthens us

to endure them. Let us then

let the flames of our passion release

the captured songs in our heart.

These songs and melodies have been stored

away to sing praises to our God

for all He has done for us.

It's the songs from the fire

that are most effective, most remembered,

and most beautifully sung.

—Dee Kamp

(*Strength for Today, Hope for Tomorrow*)

* * *

The Lord is close to those whose hearts are breaking.

Psalm 34:18 TLB

Cam, my
business
partner

Cam with new cars we had just added to our fleet.

~ 11 ~

The Anguish of My Soul 1998

My son worked with me one Monday and then was in heaven the next Monday. The day after Cam's funeral, I functioned on auto-pilot at our office. If the fog lifted for a few seconds, Cam's seven day hospital stay rushed into my mind pushing me to my knees in agony.

Cam's office stood silent. One week before, laughter had filled our rental offices. We were planning to build a cabin on the property we owned in the Colorado wilderness.

As I opened Cam's desk drawer, the plans came tumbling out. I could hear Cam's voice saying, "Mom, a gate with LAZY C hung high on posts, and then we'll drive through the aspen grove to our log cabin."

The LAZY C won't happen. In my private pain, I fingered the papers. *Where will these dreams go to die? Where can I go to die?*

We'd planned our family business venture to be passed on to future generations. I would pass Dirt Cheap to Cameron, and he to his son. *What good is a plan without a dream? Cam, you made dreams come true. Please don't be gone. Come home. Life could be perfect again.*

I needed to grieve. My heart demanded it. The first night after his death, I took a sleeping pill and had a horrendous nightmare. In the vivid scene, I saw myself being sucked out into the ocean. No boat, no Cameron, only a wooden plank. I grabbed the plank and hung on until my muscles hurt and my red, bloody fingers ached. Finally, my body numbed. Blackness enfolded everything. No one heard my screams. The floating ice cut me. I could not handle the torture of the waves.

I knew I could drown in sorrow and deep depression. I needed to stay positive and fight, but I was overwhelmed. I'd lost my dad, Lou and Gay who raised me, my grandparents, and a brother, and I'd recovered. This grief for my son seemed never ending. I wanted to die. But as a Christian, I felt ashamed of those feelings. Rest came for a few minutes, and only when I put myself under the wings of my heavenly Father. *I have hope. But how can I make it through each day? Someday we'll be together in heaven—but what about today?*

Dirt Cheap Car Rental 1998

The company choked down $50,000 to $60,000 a month just to pay the bills. Like powering an old locomotive, we shoveled cash into our business. The locomotive pushed straight ahead with a force nothing could stop. Cameron had been the engineer. Now I was in this place of torment. I wanted to run away and hide, but the company must keep running.

Cam, watching from above, would have been proud of me. All the cars were rented out. He would have given me a thumbs-up. On Cam's executive desk his small clock still sat silent. The hands pointed to the exact time his heart beat for the last time.

Lord, why should I place a new battery into Cam's clock? Time stands still. Why should his little clock keep ticking?

His big executive chair sat so high my feet did not touch the floor. Organizing his paperwork, I opened the top drawer and found our five-year-plan for opening more car rental offices.

Cam had driven his black Porsche home with full intentions of driving back to work the next day. His Cross pen lay on the paperwork left on his desk. He was planning to order twenty new cars.

Years after his death, letters still came addressed to Mr. Cameron G. Christman.

Don't people know? Don't people everywhere understand? Cam is not here anymore and won't be coming back.

My tears caused the ink on the envelopes to run and blur.

Every day, driving to our office, I'd still wonder, *would Cam be behind his desk?*

Something else kept my cheeks wet all day: Susan would give birth to their baby in five months. Cam would never hug his baby.

Help me, God, I can't breathe. My heart is broken.

Fly and Crash 1998

The open door invites a bird into our office building. The sparrow flies around in Cam's office and then dips through the doorway into my area.

Little and fearful, the bird can't see the blue sky and does not know the way to freedom.

Lord, be with the little one, slow him down so he doesn't hurt himself. Let me catch him.

One, two, three thuds, the precious bird crashes against my office window and falls to the floor. His body heaves, his beak opens and closes in fast pants.

"Soon you will be free," I said, as I reach down, and pick up my feathered friend. We walk to the door.

"Chirp—chirp—chirp," the bird sings. My hand opens. The sparrow's wings carry his brown and white body into the air, free.

Hope is a thing with feathers that perches in the soul

and sings the tune without the words

and never stops at all.

Emily Dickinson

After the bird's release, I stop, look into Cam's unused office, walk in, and push his chair tight to the desk. "Cam, I miss you."

Cam's mild cologne lingers. My eyes search his office for clues of his last week at work. The pictures on the wall speak only of his life in the fast lane. In the last picture Susan took of him, he sat in his black Porsche securing the five-way racing harness. There is a smile on his face.

In the next picture of Cam, he wears an orange jumpsuit, skydiving into the wild blue yonder.

* * *

Cam often said, "I'll buy, you fly, Mom. Pick us up steak sandwiches."

Back at the office, Cam's long legs rested on the top of his desk, we'd laugh and eat lunch together.

* * *

Now, alone at our office, I rent cars and run to answer the phone. "Will Cam be at the next Porsche Club meeting?" the caller asks.

What? My hand covered the receiver, sobbing, catching my breath.

"Cameron died two weeks ago of acute leukemia," I reply. No use to say more. There is nothing more to be said.

What do I fear?

My wings are broken. My grief is deep. My wound so raw, maybe I'll never be carefree to fly again. Love has no end. My son's name is carved on my heart.

After the death of Cameron, anguish and grief take up residence and live inside me. They turn when I turn, sleep when I sleep, walk when I walk, ride with me in my car. The minute my eyes open, they are there to devour me.

I spiral into the center of the emotional storm. God knows I cannot fly by myself. He picks me up, cradles me in His hands. Together, we plunge through the storm. I recognize it's the only way to get to the other side.

A Faithful Christian

"Cam, the most important thing in life to me is not how many cars we have on rent, but that my sons are with me in heaven."

He'd just roll his eyes at me.

Every time I found a book I thought he should read, I'd put it on his desk after he left the office. Sometimes the book appeared back on my desk the next day, many books disappeared forever.

One day on my way out the door to make marketing calls, Cam held up a book with the picture of a young Billy Graham on the cover.

"Mom, there is a chapter in this book I really believe. As a matter of fact, I'm going to take it home for Susan to read."

Two weeks later Cam died.

I called Susan, "Could you look for a book with a picture of Billy Graham on the blue cover? Please bring it along the next time you come to the office."

The book, *The Faithful Christian*, was still in his car. One of Cam's business cards, CGC Enterprises, marked a chapter titled "The Answer."

Susan brought the book to me.

I clutched the book realizing part of me died when Cam died. There was no new part to put in my body. Cam was irreplaceable.

My mind returned to times before he died. Hugging the book, I was still hanging onto him. I knew these were the words he read and believed just two weeks before he died.

Where Is Cam?

Pastor Miles words still haunted me, "Cam is on the fence and could go either way."

After I finished work one night, I walked into Cam's office and fell on my knees with my face on the floor, pleading, "God, here I am again, needing a word of wisdom. Where did my darling son end up at the end of his earthly voyage? Tell me again, God, that he's with You."

The next morning something miraculous happened. My son, Del, stationed in Germany, had Christian friends all over the world. One of these friends, Kelley, an Air Force pilot's wife in Australia, wrote my son a letter. In it she said, "During my prayer time for Cam, I envisioned Jesus coming to Cam while he was in a coma and asking him, 'Why have you kicked against Me and denied Me for so long?' And Cameron responded, 'My God, You really are He! Why would I choose anything else, I choose to go with You, Jesus.'"

Kelley continued,

"Another lady, Jill, had been praying for Cam. The day before Cam died, Jill knew in her heart something significant had happened. Cameron was going to be all right. Not necessarily allowed to live, but all right with the Lord. She sensed peace."

Kelley also sent me Jill's words, "I'm writing you on the prompting of the Holy Spirit, and hope it will bring peace to the heart and soul and spirit of those involved. As I got the facts from Kelley about Cameron, and an extra prompting from God to pray, I immediately took the request to my prayer closet. My concerns were his salvation, his wife's strength, the unborn baby, and the effect and impact he made on his family and friends.

"It seems in life Cameron touched a lot of people. He touched God's heart too. I felt I had broken through to the throne room and I was kneeling before God. His comfort and love spoke deeply to me. I asked if He would visit Cameron and let him have an experience only God could give. That he would be given a revelation and choice, that Jesus would come to him and call him by name 'Cameron' and talk to him.

"I had it all that day, the faith, the hope, the evidence! It is an experience I will never forget.

"God wants none to perish. I believe with all my heart God visited Cameron while he was in the coma. I believe God spent time with him and Cameron could not pass up the decision of his lifetime. He had a choice to be with Jesus. I believe he made the right choice too."

Can you imagine two people in different parts of the world both knowing Cam had gone into a coma? At the same time Jill and Kelley were praying, I believe the Lord Jesus came to Cam at Scripps Green Hospital.

Hope for the Dark Days

I am worn out with pain;

every night my pillow is

wet with tears.

Psalm 6:6 TLB

To all who mourn ... he will give:

Beauty for ashes; joy instead of mourning;

praise instead of heaviness.

Isaiah 61:3 TLB

God is gracious—it is he who makes things right,

our most compassionate God.

God takes the side of the helpless;

when I was at the end of my rope,

he saved me.

Psalm 116:6 The Message

~ 12 ~

The Box Is Given Wings 1998

The box was heavier than I expected. My arms barely reached around it. With my fingers locked, it was still hard to carry. Clutching the metal container to my chest, fear of loss rose up within me and shot thru my heart. Some tragedies are too big for a heart to hold. This was one of them.

The weight of my loss could only be measured by my heart. *How is it possible for so much precious matter to fit into such a small space?* I couldn't hold the question in my thoughts without my body trembling.

My tears dried, making my cheeks tight and itchy. My heart started pounding and my body welled up for more crying. A cloud of depression descended on me as one loud bellow was forced from my pit of despair. *Ohhhhh, Loooord.*

A few days earlier, I'd called Susan asking about Cam's remains. Susan wanted his ashes scattered at sea.

"Oh no, please don't scatter his ashes. I desperately need somewhere to tend him," I sobbed. "The stormy waves crashing on the rocks; the water would be too cold for my baby. I love walking by the edge of the sea. If the only part left of my beloved son was spread on the water, I could no longer enjoy sunsets over the ocean." I snuffled gulps of air and held back tears.

Susan said "the box" was in one of Cam's favorite spots, on the car seat behind the steering wheel of his black Porsche.

"Our manager, Ed, will pick up Cam's remains tomorrow morning. He'll bring the box to the office. Jerry will help me to pick out a plot and headstone," I said.

Susan agreed. She knew the closeness of mom and son.

The day after I talked to Susan, my Volvo climbed the steep rise of the Coronado Bridge which crossed San Diego Bay. My whole world felt shattered. My eyes were sore and red. I had wept with heart-rending, uncontrollable sobs all night.

Crazy thoughts were going through my head as my car edged its way to the top of the bridge: *So what if I lose control of my car? I've lost control of my life.* My thoughts weren't about the crash hurting me or the car falling from the bridge. I didn't care.

"Would my car float? Would the cabin of the car be crushed flat?" I talked to myself. My thoughts weren't about my husband. He is strong. He'll miss me, but his faithful words were always, "Life goes on."

Cam's baby in Susan's belly hasn't been born. *How could the baby miss me?*

Then, loving thoughts of my oldest son, Del, flooded into my mind, "He needs me!"

The bridge curved over the Bay and slowly sloped into the traffic jam on Interstate 5. Arriving at our office I'd normally stride into Dirt Cheap, knowing the day would be full of work and planning to open more offices. The first person I usually saw was my son. "Hi, Mom" were the first words I'd hear.

On this morning, I crept up the steps and slowly opened the front door. I peeked at Ed sitting behind the rental desk.

"Where's Cam?" I sobbed.

Ed pointed to the storage room. I walked through my office and into the back area. I could barely make out the black metal box sitting in a corner of the old gold couch. The only light in the room was coming from the open door I'd just walked through.

I sat down at the opposite end of the couch, as far away from this foreign object as possible. All my loved ones were placed in caskets when they died. I'd never seen a cremation box. My eyes studied the size and shape of the box. *How is it possible this is all that remains of my handsome son?*

I moved closer and ran my fingers over and around the hard box. Dread crept up my spine.

* * *

The box remained in my office four days, while we waited for our appointment at El Camino Cemetery. I stayed in the back room most of the time struggling with thoughts about Cam. I was alone. Del, in the Air Force, had flown back to Germany. We've no relatives living in California, and there's no community to which I belong in San Diego.

My arms were holding Cameron for the last time here on earth. During those four days, my soul felt completely shattered.

* * *

When either Cam or I didn't want to do something we'd say, "Not really." Cam's remains are buried by the lake at El Camino Cemetery. His grave marker reads: Not really. Cam is not here, Cam is in heaven.

I walked in the sunshine to Cameron's grave, but saw only the shadows of this unexpected journey. First, I cut the grass around the grave marker with scissors. Kneeling with a toothbrush and soapy water, I cleaned the nameplate, CAMERON G. CHRISTMAN.

On the sides of the headstone are pictures of mountains covered with pine trees, like the area of Colorado where we'd planned for the Lazy C Ranch to be built.

From Cam's gravesite, I watched frogs on lily pads and ducks swimming with their babies. I stood in silence and then sat on the thick, dark green grass by his grave.

My world still crashes down around me, my body shakes and heaves with sobs.

Leaving the cemetery after visiting Cam's grave, I focus on past occasions when Jerry, Cam, and I stayed at the Marriott Resort in Palm Desert. My balcony lounge chair overlooked the golf course. Reading my book, I'd hear, "Hi, Mom, watch me make this shot!" from Cam. Looking up, there was my boy. His sun bleached hair matched his tan.

"Good shot," I'd say, as I watched him walk out of sight.

Cameron, in his twenties, wasn't going with a girl, so we spent lots of time together working and playing.

A picture of Cam in a big bright striped sweater graces my desk. Jerry and Cam stand with their arms resting on the mantel of the fireplace. They had just finished a round of golf at Palm Desert.

* * *

On the second anniversary of Cam going to heaven, Jerry and our brother in the Lord, Pastor Bill Rudge, went with me to Cam's grave site. Bill gave me a set of praying hands made of wood from Jerusalem. Bill told me, "Kc, many people will be led to the Lord, through your testimony, because of Cameron's death."

Bill penned these words on the card: "The Lord spoke to my heart to give you these praying hands from the old city of Jerusalem. The Lord impressed that they should remind you to keep praying and trusting. Restoration! One day your hands and Cameron's will be together again. Look up, just as the fingers of the hands point heavenward, always keep your eyes on Jesus."

Hope for the Dark Days

The mind can descend far lower than the body ... flesh can

bear only a certain number of

wounds and no more, but the soul can

bleed in ten thousand ways and die

over and over again each hour.

—Charles Spurgeon

For I know that my Redeemer lives,

and He shall stand at last on the earth;

and after my skin is destroyed,

this I know, that in my flesh I shall see God,

whom I shall see for myself,

and my eyes shall behold, and not another.

How my heart yearns within me!

Job 19:25-27 NKJV

Jerry and Cam (in his striped sweater) after a round of golf in Desert Springs

Section Four
The Rest of the Story

~ 13 ~

Cloud in Mexico 1998

*J*erry and I were scheduled for a Christmas trip to Cancun. The season meant to be *jolly* found not one *jolly* bone in my tired old body. This was December. Cameron died in May.

"OK, Jerry, stop asking," I said. "I'm going with you to Mexico. I don't want to go, I don't want to stay, and I don't want to ever do anything again! I'm not leaving my room down there with these red eyes."

On Friday, we boarded the plane. I took the aisle seat and dozed while people were boarding. We were in the air when my eyes opened.

"Jerry, why have they seated them so close to us?" I looked across the aisle at a young, good looking man with his son. The man must have been over six-feet tall. The little boy, dressed in blue, jumped up and down on his daddy's lap. The man put his baseball cap on backwards to keep the baby from grabbing the brim.

Oh dear Lord, that should be Cameron with his son.

Severe depression set in. I closed my eyes. Curling up next to my husband and looking the other way, I dreamed sweet things as the jet engine lulled me to sleep. In my dream, Cameron won his battle with acute leukemia.

* * *

Our airplane landed in Cancun. The lucky man across the aisle slowly put his son's arms into the sleeves of the small jacket and walked down the aisle to get off the airplane. I struggled to hold back the tears.

Why was Cameron robbed of never seeing his son? Give me one reason, Lord.

After we checked into our Marriott hotel room, it was time for watching the waves. Wave after wave slid back and forth onto the sand, each wave bringing heartache and intense personal pain.

After a couple of days, Jerry walked into our room, scrunched his face to sympathize and said, "The day is sunny and hot, get your swimming suit on and come to the beach with me. Your choice: walk or I will carry you."

Jerry found me a beach chair in the sand. He ran out to the waves and began swimming in the ocean.

Sitting and pouting, I talked to the Lord. "I'm hurting and angry at You for letting my son die. You owe me something, Lord. I want to know what Cameron is doing today."

Keeping my eyes closed for several minutes, I repeated over and over in my demanding voice, "I want to see what Cameron is doing right now! Show me!"

Opening my eyes, I looked to the sky and saw the clouds above me formed into unmistakable pictures of:

- Cameron sitting in the seat of his Porsche

- His long arms stretched out

- His hands on the round steering wheel

- Cam's profile with a smile

- Cam's baseball cap on backwards

- His long legs on the foot pedal

- Behind his head were long streams of clouds. To me they symbolized the extreme speed he'd found in heaven.

I stared at the formation of the man in the big white, puffy cloud. "Thanks, Lord, for placing a bandage over my open wound. Never again will I beg you for a sign."

Smiling, and then looking up at the cloud, I spoke softly, "Slow down, Honey, slow down."

Riding with Cameron, I often said: "Slow down, Honey, you'll get another speeding ticket."

* * *

That night God gave me a dream which soothed and relaxed my tired, weary body. In my dream, I stood on a dock. Alongside the dock appeared a white boat with my son laying in it. A white, downy blanket covered Cameron. His eyes were shut; his facial expression peaceful.

Pushing the boat away from the dock into the lake, I bawled.

"I'll never see you again," I murmured.

The further the boat drifted away from me, the sadder I became. Then God revealed to me what happened on the other side of the lake.

When the white boat arrived on the far shore, Cameron stepped out of the boat, and pulled it ashore. Then Jesus and my son embraced, as Jesus said, "Welcome home, Cam, welcome home."

All my loved ones who had died were also on the shore to welcome Cam home.

"Hi," said my dad, Albert, "you must be Karen's son, Cameron. I never met you on earth. Welcome to heaven." The last thing I saw in my dream was my dad giving Cam a big hug.

This dream didn't give me an answer as to why God allowed Cam to die, nor did it end all of my grief. But I was experiencing another lesson about the sovereignty of God, and understanding that the peace He offers doesn't necessarily come with the answers to all of our questions.

The next morning I told Jerry, "The Lord gave me a blessed assurance in my dream that Cam is not stuck in the grave. Book me a bus ticket and I'll go with you tomorrow to the Mayan ruins."

All day when I thought of the vision the Lord gave me in the sky, I thought of what King David said, *The clouds are his chariots. He rides upon the wings of the wind"* (Psalm 104:3 TLB).

Hope for the Dark Days

My help and glory are in God—

granite-strength and safe-harbor-God—

So trust him absolutely, people;

lay your lives on the line for him.

God is a safe place to be.

Psalm 62:7-8 The Message

I'm asking God for one thing,

only one thing:

To live with him in his house

my whole life long.

I'll contemplate his beauty;

I'll study at his feet.

Psalm 27:4 The Message

~ 14 ~

Cameron Cole

usan, my daughter-in-law, invited me to go with her for the sonogram. The doctor said, "Look it's a baby boy. He is giving a thumbs-up." My heart started pounding. I felt like life drained away from me. I heard Cameron's voice say, "Good job Mom."

At Dirt Cheap Car Rental when Cam said, "Good job," I'd look at him and he'd give me a thumbs-up. Almost every week when things were rolling, Cameron would give me a thumbs-up. His unborn baby boy just bestowed on me a thumbs-up.

Susan gave me a framed picture of the baby doing a thumbs-up, just like his daddy in heaven. The sonogram picture stayed on my desk to help me work through the finality of my loss.

Cameron Cole Christman (Cole) came into the world on October 25, 1998, perfect in every way.

When Cole was nine years old, I took him to Chuck E. Cheese. Cole was sitting on a seat playing a racing game. I froze as I looked at Cole. It was the exact image I had seen in the clouds of his dad during my trip to Cancun, Mexico.

Every year Susan takes Cole to his dad's grave. On the twelfth anniversary of Cam's death, Cole released twelve balloons to honor his daddy in heaven. Red, purple, black, yellow balloons brightened the sky.

Fly away to heaven … fly. One balloon for every year of not seeing, and feeling, and playing, and laughing, and loving, and eating, and sleeping, and praying, and camping, and surfing, and skiing, and kicking the football with his dad.

There are many more "ands" that Cole will never experience with his father.

Hope for the Dark Days

We can hug our hurts and make a shrine out
of our sorrows or we can offer them to God
as a sacrifice of praise. The choice is ours.

— Richard Exley

Don't panic. I'm with you.
There's no need to fear for I'm your God.
I'll give you strength. I'll help you.
I'll hold you steady, keep a firm grip on you.

Isaiah 41:10 The Message

Since we believe that Jesus died and then
came back to life again, we can also believe
that when Jesus returns, God will bring back
with him all the Christians who have died.

1 Thessalonians 4:14 TLB

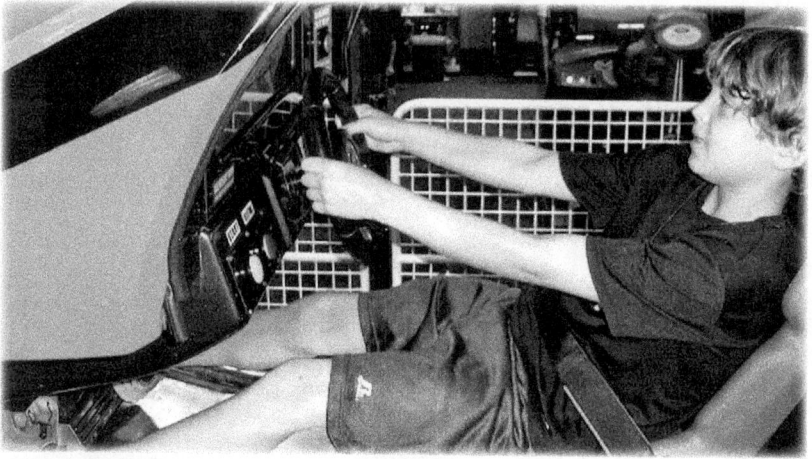

Cole playing an arcade game. (This picture is so much like the image of Cam I saw in the clouds in Cancun.)

Susan remarried and had two more children. (*Left to right*) Valerie, Susan, Quinn, and Cole.

~ 15 ~

Del

September 11, 2001—just another routine day, or so we thought. I pushed the coffeepot "on" button and turned on *Good Morning America* to glimpse smoke billowing from one of the World Trade Center buildings!

"What? What's happening?" I gasped.

"Hurry," I yelled to Jerry, "a plane crashed into a building in New York."

Time stood still for us. Then a second jet crashed. Both World Trade Center buildings were on fire. We weren't capable of lifting our coffee cups.

Death came to so many sitting at their desks. People were trapped in a burning inferno with no warning. Like millions of others around the world, Jerry and I sat glued to our TV. Our nation was gripped by the sight of thousands of people wandering the streets of lower Manhattan.

During the terrorist attack, I said, "Jerry, do you think this is the end of the world?"

The pictures were straight from hell—people falling to their deaths! A third jet crashed into the Pentagon leaving a gaping, smoking hole.

Del's office was in the Pentagon. This third assault on our nation just became personal. I frantically searched to find out what happened at the Pentagon attack.

"Del, answer your phone!" I screamed. He didn't.

I called Del's wife. "Beth, Beth, your phone, answer it." She didn't.

A recording came on: "All lines are busy, please call again later."

The weight of depression pressing on me since Cam's death felt heavier!

Lord God, this can't be happening again. Not another son! There is no way I can sink any deeper in this emotional quicksand that surrounds me...and still live.

The phone rang.

"Kc, a customer needs to talk to you about making several car reservations for the F.B.I. How soon can you be at the office?" Ed asked.

Time goes by faster when you're busy. In my panic, I grabbed my cell phone and flung my address book into my purse as I ran out the door. "Honey, as soon as there's any news, I'll call you."

At the office, the TV kept showing all the unbelievable destruction and gut-wrenching scenes. My phone never left my hand.

Beth's father, Maurice, had been in the military. He

might know of some way to reach Del during this national disaster. I called Maurice and Lida. They weren't home.

Unable to reach my son, my blood pressure soared. As a mother, I'd done everything to insure my sons' safety when they were young: seat belts, child-proof caps, holding their hands when crossing streets, warning them about talking to strangers.

Earnestly praying, I recognized Del was in God's hands.

Throughout the day, thoughts of Del came creeping in every few minutes. He'd accepted the Lord while at the Air Force Academy, married a Christian woman, and had three wonderful Christian children, Sarah, Joshua, and Hannah.

Del started his Air Force career as a Northrop T-38 Talon instructor pilot in Undergraduate Pilot Training (UPT). He went on to be an aircraft commander and instructor pilot in the Boeing E-3 AWACS, short for Airborne Warning and Control System. While in AWACS, Del flew over one hundred combat missions in the Gulf during Operations Desert Storm and Provide Comfort. He later went on to fly with NATO AWACS during operations in Bosnia and Kosovo.

I did not know what his full duties were at the Pentagon, but I imagined him in a war room where military men and women were trying to keep our skies safe. My mind was totally exhausted with worry.

Much later in the day, Beth finally managed to call me back. "Del is safe! He was in the Pentagon during the attack. But the building is enormous and his office hasn't been damaged."

He'd managed to slip a quick phone call to Beth, "Honey, I'm OK, but I'm going to be working late tonight." That had to be the understatement of the century.

Beth relayed to me, "Del won't be able to call you for a few days as everyone is extremely busy at the Pentagon."

People working in the Pentagon who were deemed non-essential were evacuated, but all personnel associated with the Air Force Crisis Action Team and Battle Staff stayed behind. Del was one of those people. He would work for the next three days in a burning building.

Del and other military leaders were busy coordinating with the Office of the President; the North American Defense Command (NORAD); the Joint Chiefs of Staff, and Combatant commanders around the world. They grounded all civilian aircraft flying over the US, diverted other airplanes inbound to the US, and coordinated combat aircraft to fly combat patrol over US soil to protect our skies. The skies, normally filled with the bustle of thousands of airplanes became eerily quiet.

Del later recounted the events from inside the Pentagon that morning. He witnessed the second aircraft hit the second tower of the World Trade Center while taking phone calls from the FAA, NORAD, and others—tracking many potential hijacked aircraft across the country, fortunately there were only four. Looking up at the television monitor from within the Air Force's Command and Control facility, he saw a news report showing the Pentagon on fire.

When did that happen? he wondered.

Only after staring for a surreal minute or two did the word at the bottom of the screen "LIVE" sink in. The Pentagon had been hit as well.

Shortly after, the fire alarms in the Pentagon started going off. He and others did what needed to be done. While Del was on what they referred to as the "bat phone," he got more disturbing news: There is another aircraft inbound to Washington DC.

Will the Pentagon be hit again?

Del told us this was the first time he'd ever really felt fear, even in light of all the combat time he'd experienced in wars on two continents.

But as he prayed there in the Pentagon, the peace only God could provide came over him. Del said he thanked God for the comfort, walked into the classified briefing room, and informed the Secretary and Chief of Staff of the Air Force of the inbound aircraft.

On my knees I prayed, "Thank you, my Father, my God, for saving the life of my son. I could not have carried the cross of a second child taken from my arms."

A fourth hijacked plane, most likely targeted for the White House or the Capitol building crashed in an open field in Pennsylvania. Stories played on TV about Todd Beamer and other passengers on the airplane saying, "Let's roll."

They tried taking the cockpit over from the terrorists. They died trying. However, many lives on the ground were saved. Todd was someone's son!

All glimmer of hope for survivors dissipated as days, and then weeks went by. It became apparent no other people would be found alive.

One hundred ten stories of concrete and steel disintegrated into six stories of soot and twisted metal. When our nation thought it could weep no more, another memorial service, another loved one would be missed.

After Cam's death I experienced a new range of emotions, my compassion for others grew. I wept with moms, dads, brothers, sisters, husbands, and wives receiving phone calls about their loved ones.

I knew sorrow from Cam's death. Now I could feel the world's pain. I found myself more alive to the present moment.

King David knew the Lord when he said: *"You've kept track of my every toss and turn through the sleepless nights: each tear entered in your ledger, each ache written in your book"* (Psalm 56:8 The Message).

Those words worked for me. God knew not only my suffering, but all the people who suffered during September, 2001.

* * *

The most astonishing rental experience happened after the 9/11 attack on the World Trade Center. Listening to the names on TV—some sounded familiar. I called Greg, at the F.B.I. office, who I had previously done investigative work for. I asked him to send me a copy of suspected terrorists who might have lived in San Diego.

Late after all my employees left work, I sat alone in my dark office, the only light coming from the computer screen. *Wham,* one of the suspected terrorists names popped up on the screen.

My body covered with goose bumps. I rented a sports car to a terrorist. The rental contract documents included the terrorist's signature and picture ID. A handsome, dark-skinned man stared back at me from his passport picture. His eyes loomed black and lifeless. I remembered this renter: he hated negotiating with a woman. He showed me his AMEX card and paid $3,500 cash for a three month rental.

We asked every renter which university or language school they attended in case we needed to reach them. This gentleman answered with a smile, "I'm taking flying lessons at Montgomery field."

Hope for the Dark Days

Now faith is the substance of things hoped

for, the evidence of things not seen.

Hebrews 11:1 KJV

Beth and Del at a military function

~ 16 ~

You Can't Go Home 2009

After twenty-five years away from North Dakota, I felt a deep need to walk on the soil where I played as a little girl. You often hear "once you leave your childhood home, you can never return and find it as you left it."

My airplane arrived in Minot around midnight in 2009. For the last twelve years in San Diego, my emotions had run deep and my burdens were heavy. Now I was beginning to glimpse rainbows at certain times.

The sun shone and the air seemed crisp as a fall apple. Strong winds blowing from Canada gave North Dakota pollution free air. Trees changed their appearance in preparation for a white winter.

"Sis, order a sixteen-ounce vanilla latte for me. You try one," I said, as LuJean drove us through Starbucks.

It's hard for me to say Minot and Starbucks in the same sentence. Drive-through coffee shops were non-existent when my teenage sons and I lived here.

Minot, now a first class city, even has a WalMart. Our hot coffee cups warmed our hands, country music played on the radio. We opened our windows halfway for nature's air-conditioning.

"Kc, I know you want to drive by Lou and Gay's farmstead," LuJean said. Gravel stones crunched under the car tires as a cloud of dust left a telltale trail. "I have to warn you, it's not the same. Neighbors bought the old homestead and are farming the land."

Busy visiting, I was not watching the road. LuJean stopped in a driveway. Looking around, nothing looked familiar. "Sis, why have we stopped?" I asked.

LuJean looked at me and frowned, "This is the farm where you grew up."

"What? It can't be," I said. "There are no buildings! Where are the trees?"

LuJean looked at me, "Kc, you lived here."

I squinted. Nothing was in sight except two round, grey, steel, grain bins.

* * *

I thought back to my life on the farm. Lou, Gay, and I would drive, walk, ride bikes, and shovel snow out of the driveway. Our white house was set back 200 feet from the road.

As a little girl, I stood in front of the huge picture window and watched for the mailman. At night when neighbors drove into the yard, their car headlights lit up the living room. I'd jump in the air and yell, "Company, company!"

Off to the left should be a red grain elevator. Sixty years ago the elevator operated like the big ones in town. Cups on a pulley automatically took the grain up and dumped it into your choice of bins. My Aunt and I crawled into the bins and shoveled the grain to the back corners. One day a mouse ran up Lou's leg under her pants.

"Help, hit my leg with a shovel, a mouse, mousseeee!" She never went back into the bins again. From then on, it always happened to be my turn.

Between the grain elevator and the house sat a long white building. The first part was a bunk house for hired men; and then came the tool shed; next the tractor garage. Flowering vines hung on the white fence at the end of the building, hiding the outhouse.

The bunk house, no longer used for hired help, became my secret playhouse during my grade school years. In the corner sat an old Victrola with rows of thick, black phonograph records in the cabinet. I passed many hours cranking and listening.

On the right stood a large red barn for cows and horses. By the windmill, I kept a tin cup for drinking cold water on hot summer days.

Hen house? Pig barn? Where did everything go?

* * *

There was no way I could believe my sister's words. This simply could not have been where I spent sixteen years riding horses through the trees and making rabbit and pigeon houses.

Slowly, I opened my car door and walked to where the house would have sat on its foundation. Pretending, I stood at the location of the north kitchen window and looked toward where the Beggs' farm should be. Just before the land dropped off, the Beggs' barn and house appeared. Tears rolled down my cheeks.

Lake Nettie came into view on the right. The lake used to be large. We skated and tobogganed down the hill onto the lake. Now it looked small, lonely, and barren—more a pond than a lake.

"Where are the shelter belts? You would have thought the people who purchased the farm could have spared the trees," I mumbled.

The wild fox, pheasants, grouse, and rabbits needed the trees for escaping the cold, wild winter winds and snowstorms. How much crop land is enough?

Crying my way through the stubble field back to the car, I said, "LuJean, wow! This is the driveway. But everything has been stripped away. Not one tree left. The huge cottonwood over 150 years old—gone!"

Sis backed her car onto the country road. We headed to Turtle Lake for hamburgers.

"Nothing! There is nothing left to tell me Lou, Gay, and I lived on this piece of land. LuJean, it doesn't bother me that the buildings are gone. You can't keep empty buildings from falling down. The missing trees are what really make me sad."

North Dakota is flat and bare. Shelter belts are planted to corral snow in the winter and prevent dirt from blowing across the roads in the summer.

Uncle Gay told me, "During the dust bowl years, in the 1930's, dust piled up like snow banks. Some days, the barn could not be seen because of all the dirt in the air."

LuJean gave me more information, "To get rid of the house, it was set on fire and burned itself into the basement."

Those words carried a punch for me. As a little girl, many nights I'd fallen asleep wondering: *If Gay's cigarette sets the house on fire, how can I escape?*

The small windows in the basement were not large enough to crawl through.

Could the house fall down on me? I wondered.

We finished our lunch at the café and headed for Strawberry Lake. Speechless, I sat in the cloud of dust our car was stirring up. For the next twenty miles, unrecognizable terrain whizzed by outside the car window.

Dorothy

I never asked Mom for her side of the story about why Lou hated her. It was a subject I just couldn't bring up. Since I couldn't prove any of Lou's allegations, the story died.

Finally when I was thirty-years-old, I needed my birth mother, Dorothy, to tell me about her past.

"How did you meet Dad?" I asked.

"My alcoholic stepdad wouldn't come home for supper. My mother, Lydia, sent me into the bar to bring him out. 'Wally, supper. Come on, hurry up,' I'd say. Many times he needed to finish his drink. I sat around and waited," Mother said. "Albert asked me, 'Are you old enough to be in my bar?' He owned the bar, and happened to be very handsome. I was fifteen years old, Al about thirty-two."

Mom got pregnant at sixteen and married Albert. Like bullets shot out of a gun, there were one, two, three, four, five children.

I realized Mom started a family when she should have been playing with dolls.

* * *

After I'd talked with Mom, I remembered, *"Honor your father and your mother that you may have a long, good life in the land the Lord your God will give you"* (Exodus 20:12 TLB).

The Lord told me, "Forgive her."

I did and started calling or writing her every month.

God's plan for me had taken a bend in the road. Even though I had been given away, Mom could have aborted me. She chose life for me.

One of my friends always raved about her mother: how much they loved each other, the shopping, hair appointments, and trips. She didn't know that from childhood my mom left me with deep wounds—they never healed.

* * *

I was still upset about all traces of my childhood home, the farm, being gone. Both Aunt Lou and Uncle Gay were also gone.

This trip to North Dakota might still bring healing if I could spend some time with Dorothy. She was living in a senior citizen home. Her second husband, Orville, had died.

LuJean and I decided Mom would love a day at Lake Metigoshe. We picked her up and drove to my niece Kathy's house. We sat visiting on Kathy's patio by the lake.

All at once Mom said, "I have to get back to Minot. Gaylin is having a potluck and hamburger fry at the senior citizen home. We need to hurry."

We knew nothing of Mom's commitment. Our only plan was watching the sunset with Kathy and her husband, Bob.

I told LuJean, "I'll sit in the back seat with Mother. I haven't visited much with her in twenty-five years." Mom and I crawled into the back seat.

Mom said, "Oh, I'm just sick. Everyone will miss me at the potluck. Hurry, drive faster, Jeanie."

"Mom, how do you like your new home at The View? Your bedroom window faces west, how are the sunsets?" I asked.

Mom ignored me. "LuJean, call so everyone knows I am on the way," she said.

"How many friends do you have? Do you play whist?" I asked.

"What time is it? Oh, I hope the people are still at the potluck," Mom said.

Arriving at The View, LuJean opened the tailgate and retrieved Mom's walker. Mom slipped out of the car as fast as an eighty-five-year-old can. She slammed the door and never said goodbye or turned around to wave.

"I love you, Mom," I choked, "I wish you could have loved me." I sat alone in the backseat.

But this time, I moved to the front seat and waited for my sister. My deepest need was to make sense out of my childhood. My sister, LuJean, loved me and showed me in many ways. I treasured days spent with her, the days we missed growing up in different homes.

* * *

I don't remember kissing or hugging Dorothy until I was sixty-eight and Mom eighty-eight. This hug happened on my next trip.

Thank you, Lord, for time with Mom.

We hugged on this trip; it was sweet—me on my knees, Mom in her wheelchair. I received that hug, first and last. I never saw her again. Mom passed away a few months later.

The last time I saw my birth mom. Dorothy in the wheelchair and me on my knees.

The beautiful farm I grew up on in North Dakota. The trees were shelter for fox, raccoon, rabbits, and birds.

All that was left in 2009 of Uncle Gerhard's farm—two steel grain bins.

~ 17 ~

God's Still Small Voice

For over thirty-five years I'd been in the car rental business. I just went through the motions of home, work, work, home. Seven years after Cam's death, I could not sit behind his desk any longer. While driving to work during the last six months, I kept hearing a still, small voice say, "Go down the street and talk to Ted at Bargain Car Rental."

Bargain and Dirt Cheap were competitors. Finally, the voice could no longer be silenced. Driving my Volvo into Bargain's parking lot, I walked into their office.

"Is Ted here?" I asked.

A young man came to the reception area and said, "I'm John, Ted's son. My dad retired and I've taken over the business."

"John, you may think this strange, but the Lord has been telling me to stop and let you know I'm selling my company and you should buy it," I said with conviction.

The week before I stopped at Bargain, John had told his father, "I need to buy another car rental company, grow bigger, or sell my current company."

I presented the business plan and sale price to John and his wife, Joy. They prayed and then made an offer.

In escrow, everything was moving along in the direction of a smooth sale. However, a couple of months before the closing date they changed their minds. Wow, what a surprise! Maybe I heard the Lord wrong.

A business broker advertised Dirt Cheap, several people were interested. An offer to buy was made and accepted.

One afternoon, a week before the second deal was to close, John and Joy stopped at my office with their beautiful little daughter.

I told them, "The sale of Dirt Cheap closes next week. I don't understand the situation as the Lord told me you should buy it."

John said, "If the sale falls out of escrow, call me. We're still interested."

The man buying Dirt Cheap changed his mind the night before the closing. He decided to go back and work for his old company. To make a long story short, John and Joy have owned Dirt Cheap Car Rental since 2005.

John told me, "We have never regretted buying the company."

All my wonderful employees are now working with John.

It brought me to tears—John and Joy's little daughter's name: Cameron. Who knows—one day their daughter may run Dirt Cheap Car Rental.

My son, Cameron, had done extremely well in making our company the best in San Diego.

Joy and daughter, Cameron, new owners of Dirt Cheap Rental (missing from the photo is John).

~ 18 ~

God

by Cameron Gene Christman
(1994)

i will pray,

but my cries for help will only be cries for guidance from the Lord.

i will pray.

i will read.

i will do whatever it takes:

i will not follow a path not knowing where it goes,

but instead make my own path so others may follow Jesus is my guide.

Seek not the dark path to riches, but follow the path of God's love. For His light is one that shines for all eternity. For true success lies within the journey not the end.

So live life for its moments.

Amen.

Cam (age 30).

Cole (age 3). Their resemblance and similarities have never ceased to amaze me. Thank you, God.

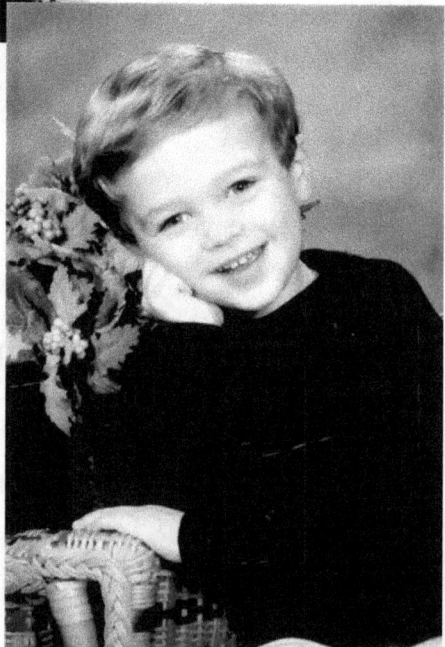

~ 19 ~

Windblown Witness

*C*am's favorite piece of mail each month was the local Porsche club magazine called, *Windblown Witness*. The month after he died, the magazine honored Cam with a cover photo of him racing his 968 black Porsche.

Skip Carter wrote in the *Windblown Witness (June 1998)*: "Cameron was the most positive, look on the good side, don't let things get you down, person I've ever met. He was the guy everyone wanted to beat. He set the standard. He exemplified the best things about our club. As a driving instructor he'd take his competitors out on the track showing them how to drive better. It never mattered he was competing against them. It was all part of the camaraderie."

* * *

I received a letter on May 22, 1998 from Suzanna, a rental customer. It said, "I knew Cameron for only five minutes—tops, but I won't ever forget him. I can only imagine how positively he affected the people who had known him for years."

Cam had given her a free car for the afternoon. She was facing a six hundred dollar repair bill on her personal car, and didn't have any money to rent a car and drive to meet some old friends.

Cameron touched many hearts.

~ 20 ~

Three Women

$\mathcal{T}$he Lord placed three women in my life who revealed I was traveling on a well-worn path: Season of Mourning.

Summer 1996

The first woman of courage is Barbara. Jerry and I were moving to a condo on the bay. In my backyard stood my wonderful aviary, which I needed to get rid of. Plus, I needed to find good homes for the birds.

Mentioning this at Bible study, someone gave me Barbara's phone number and told me she loved birds. She bred parakeets and sold them, which I also had been doing.

Barbara came to my house and picked up some birds. Bragging about my sons and three grandchildren—that's what we grandmothers do—I asked, "Do you have any children?"

"My only daughter is in heaven." Barbara said. "Lenora graduated from high school and wanted to attend a local college. We were close and did everything together.

"One of Lenora's friends, Julie, wanted to make a trip to Los Angeles to pick up a friend, my daughter rode along. Their car was hit by a drunk driver while coming home. Both Julie and Lenora died at the scene, as did the drunk driver, who was going north in a southbound lane. Lenora's ashes are still on the shelf in her bedroom closet."

I'd never sat and talked to a mother who had lost a child. My emotions screamed for relief of even the thought of one of my sons dying!

In May, 1998, Barbara was the first person I called and pleaded, "Barb, Cam has been diagnosed with leukemia. Pray that my son will not die."

The two of us knew Christ held the true meaning of life. His book, the Bible, is our medicine.

Summer 1998

After Cam died, someone from our church told me to call Patti. We met at Denny's café. I remembered her story because it made the front page of the *Union Tribune* a few years prior.

Patti said, "I arrived home from church. A window gapped open. There on the floor I found my sixteen-year-old daughter stabbed to death and raped."

Tears were in her eyes as she talked about the love she had for her Father God who was sustaining her.

"It took three years to find the murderer. The man actually went back to the scene where my daughter was murdered. They caught him looking in the window of our old home, now occupied by a new mother and daughter."

Patti moved many times after her daughter's death, fearing for her life. She sat through the murderer's lies and listened to the gory, ugly details during the trial.

January 2000

The third lady worked in a cottage that sold homemade arts and craft items. Alice, a seventy-three-year-old grandmother, had eyes full of sorrow. Of course, she listened to the Cam story.

"Why are you working? You should be home with a good book on a cold winter day like this," I said.

Alice said, "My husband and I lived a full life, including raising four sons. Three days after my husband retired, he flew to Northern California to buy an airplane. On take-off, he crashed the plane into a building at the airport and died instantly.

"Four days later at my husband's grave site, my father died of a heart attack."

We were now standing crying and hugging.

She continued, "After my father died, my mother wanted out of the big city, we moved to Idyllwild.

"Within the two-week period that mom and I were moving, my twenty-six-year-old son was killed in a motorcycle accident. My son, recently divorced, had two daughters I brought into my home to raise.

Then I was sued for $4.5 million from my husband's airplane crash. We lost everything."

We were now both sobbing.

I shared, *"What does it profit a woman if she has the whole world and loses her soul?"* [author's paraphrase of Matthew 16:26]

She was a Christian and we shared our beliefs about heaven.

~ 21 ~

Things that Stay with Us

Green, rusty, and dented, the old suitcase came into the kitchen. Opening it I found: an old scrapbook started by Aunt Louise in 1938 and finished by me in the 1940's; Sears, Roebuck and Co. catalog, Fall and Winter, 1957, page 140, my dress, Sissy Shirtwaist in pretty Dan River woven plaid gingham. "Wedding-ring" collar, perky tie. Nylon ruffles edged with embroidery. Wide belt nips waist above full skirt. Washable cotton. $7.44: small leather album from the Black Hills.

* * *

Today, I'm grateful when shopping at Costco. Buying the packs of paper towels, toilet paper, and boxes of plastic bags gives me the feeling of being rich. Growing up, our plastic bags were washed out bread sacks, no paper towels, and if we ran out of toilet paper, the *Turtle Lake Journal* worked.

Sometimes we don't understand or realize why we do the things we do, or say the things we say. For example: I would never eat an apple unless it was cut into slices. I didn't know the reason. Way back in my thoughts, my mind told me...*bad apple, you're going to get punished!* I had no idea, until I was fifty-years-old, why I would not pick up and eat a whole apple.

LuJean was visiting me in Coronado. She brought two apples out to the patio. I said, "No thanks."

LuJean asked me, "Do you remember Grandma Schmidt? She would sit us on the steps to the basement and give us each an apple. We could not get up until every bit of the apple was gone. If we jumped up to play and she found part of our apple uneaten, she spanked us with the belt. I'd hide what I could not eat in a pocket or my underpants."

I must not have been that clever. Even to this day, when I eat an apple—I'll eat the apple, the seeds, the little husks around the seeds, all the inners, and then I'll chew on the stem until the only thing left is the hard nubbin on the stem. That little nubbin will stay in my mouth most of the day. I'll chew on it, even though it hurts my teeth.

* * *

Cameron's cotton striped sweater of bright blue, yellow, and green sits in an honored place in my closet. My nose buries itself in the sweater, no smell. I will keep it all my life. Each season when I'm sorting my summer/winter clothes, I slip it on and wrap my arms around myself. Size x-large, the arms hang down to my knees.

~ Afterword ~

The truth of my experiences can come only through my voice. My writings have kept my son's memory vivid. I also write to preserve the heritage of my faith that strengthens me throughout my life. I want to pass on a tradition of faith and virtue for future generations.

In 1998, I felt my heart would never sing again, but God healed my broken heart.

When my grandson Joshua was accepted into the Air Force Academy to follow in his father's (Del) footsteps...my heart sang!

At my granddaughter Sarah's pinning ceremony as a registered nurse...my heart sang!

The Bible tells us, *"Our children too shall serve him, for they shall hear from us about the wonders of the Lord; generations yet unborn shall hear of all the miracles he did for us"* (Psalms 22:30-31 TLB).

Del graduated from the Air Force Academy in 1985.

Del's son, Joshua, will graduate from the Air Force Academy in 2013.

My oldest granddaughter, Sarah, and her sister Hannah Joy

~ The Vine ~

Kc is the old vine,
Cameron is her offspring,
Jerry, Kc's husband, is the gentle oak.

Thirty years ago, the old vine was more beautiful.
It was tough when she was up-rooted in Colorado and
moved to California.

For a while, she was all alone.
Then her offspring rooted next to her.

Storms blew in from the Pacific,
But there was always sun after the storm.
Oh the joy the two shared side by side.
Look how their branches intertwine:
The offspring's branches reached much higher
Oh what a sight, the two of them.

Woven together, one couldn't tell which
Branches belonged to the old vine or offspring.

Oh no! The old vine is starting to shake.
Something was tearing the offspring away—
It was not gentle.

Strong tugs…one branch and then another,
The old vine could do nothing but whither
As the intertwined branches were ripped away.
It took only one week.

He was damaged, torn,
Oh no, he's dying, burned, cremated—
The old vine would never bloom again.

She had a hard time standing,
Even during a gentle breeze.
Most of her roots were torn out.
On the other side stood a gentle oak.

The old vine had just enough strength
And wrapped two scarred branches
Around the trunk of the gentle oak.

The gentle oak does not mind.
The tears of the old vine, mingled with love,
Tugged at the gentle oak's heartstrings.
The son/sun sets on another day.

~ Acknowledgments ~

Aunt Mary Kennerly told me, "Kc, look at this article in the Port Townsend newspaper, classes at The Writers' Workshoppe. I think some of the things you've written are excellent. You should present your work at these classes." This was my starting point. Every week, for two years, I wrote three hundred to five hundred words from my journals or words the Lord placed in my heart.

Anna Quinn (the shop's owner), Carol, Holly, (plus other women at different times) and I met weekly. We laughed and cried together. Fellow writers, you gave me the courage to tell my story.

Dee Kamp, I met during Bible study at Randi's house, read some of the chapters and said, "There definitely is a book waiting to be born." Dee has written and published two books.

Step-by-step, tear-by-tear when my mind groped for bearing in the turbulent sea, you women kept my sails tight.

My sister, LuJean, filled in the family life I missed by not growing up at home.

To you wonderful women, I say, "Thank you from the bottom of my heart. You made me feel safe enough to dig deep."

~ Endorsement ~

As you read *A Broken Heart,* you'll fall in love with the precious red-headed girl with the green tin suitcase. Kc becomes your child, sister, and friend.

I pray Kc's story will make you aware of the gentle hand of Christ as you are drawn closer to His heart and through your own dark valley into His marvelous light.

Melannie Babboni
Family Life Pastor

New Life Church
Port Townsend, Washington

~ About the Author ~

Karen (Kc) was born on the windy plains of North Dakota. She has been married twenty-eight years to the love of her life, Jerry. They live on the Olympic Peninsula in Port Townsend, Washington and attend New Life Church.

Pastimes include: her parrots (Bwana, an African Grey, and BooHoo, a Ducorp's Cockatoo), playing the piano, reading the Bible and Women's Bible studies, writing, nature walks, boating with Jerry, spending time with her six grandchildren, and vacationing with her sister, LuJean.

Proud mother of two sons: Del, retired from the Air Force, and now a professor at the Air Force Academy in Colorado Springs; Cameron, at home with the Lord in heaven.

~ The Rescue ~

All praise to the God and Father of our Master,
Jesus the Messiah! Father of
all mercy! God of all healing counsel!
He comes alongside us when we go through
hard times, and before you know it,
he brings us alongside someone else who is
going through hard times so that we
can be there for that person just as
God was there for us.

2 Corinthians 1:3-4 The Message

~ Contact Information ~

Kc Hutter

2023 E. Sims Way, #152

Port Townsend, WA 98368

hutter.kc@gmail

www.ingramcontent.com/pod-product-compliance
Lightning Source LLC
Chambersburg PA
CBHW070825100426
42813CB00003B/486